Lethal Ladies

by Lynda F

Humourous and suspenseful novels written when the world was a different place; where Good always triumphs over Evil; and clever brains discover the hidden heart of human behaviour.

Dedicated to Wendy Thom in happy memory of our shared delight in the books.

C 2004, 2017

Introduction

In 1901 The Strand Magazine serialized *"The Hound of the Baskervilles"* featuring Sherlock Holmes and ushered in the Golden Age of Detection.

Devoted readers befriended and loyally supported favourite characters. After all, it was public outcry that forced Sir Arthur Conan Doyle to bring Holmes back from Reichenbach Falls.

Mystery is a genre that attracts people who enjoy puzzles. This quiz book has more than five hundred questions to challenge the fans of Margery Allingham, Agatha Christie, Ngaio Marsh, Dorothy L. Sayers, Josephine Tey, and Patricia Wentworth *(only her Miss Silver series)*.

These questions *(taken from novels, short stories, biographies, anthologies, and autobiographies)* are divided into chapters with the answers at the end of the book along with a complete list of the resources used.

If you're stumped for an answer can you remember the book where you'll find it? Revisit and enjoy anew!

Table of Contents

Chapter 1	Addresses.....................	6
Chapter 2	Animals.......................	7
Chapter 3	Capital Punishment.......	10
Chapter 4	Careers.......................	12
Chapter 5	Cars	15
Chapter 6	Clubs	16
Chapter 7	Education....................	17
Chapter 8	Family.........................	19
Chapter 9	Friends & Cohorts.........	21
Chapter 10	Habits.........................	23
Chapter 11	Matchmaking................	26
Chapter 12	Nicknames & Aliases......	27
Chapter 13	Old Tragedies...............	30
Chapter 14	Personal Staff...............	32
Chapter 15	Personal Trivia..............	35
Chapter 16	Policemen....................	37
Chapter 17	Publications.................	39
Chapter 18	Quotes........................	43
Chapter 19	Religion.......................	45
Chapter 20	Romance......................	47
Chapter 21	Scotland Yard...............	49
Chapter 22	Sherlock Holmes...........	51
Chapter 23	Sports & Games...........	52
Chapter 24	St Mary Mead..............	53
Chapter 25	Trivial Trivia.................	55
Chapter 26	Unusual Weapons.........	58
Chapter 27	Wartime......................	59
Chapter 28	Wills & Epitaphs...........	61
Chapter 29	About the Authors.........	63
Chapter 30	The Really Tough Trivia..	67
Chapter 31	Fun With Book Titles.....	69
Chapter 32	Novels Also Known As...	71

Answers................................. 74

Works of Margery Allingham......... 145
Works of Agatha Christie.............. 149
Works of Ngaio Marsh.................. 157
Works of Dorothy L. Sayers.......... 159
Works of Josephine Tey................ 161
Works of Patricia Wentworth......... 162

Listing of Resources Used............. 164

Chapter 1 - Addresses
who lives where?

1.) 48 Regency Close

2.) 15 Montague Mansions

3.) 100 Doughty Street

4.) Duke's Denver

5.) 12a Bottle Street

6.) Tatler's End

7.) West Leaham Street

8.) 110a Piccadilly West

9.) Pontisbright Mill

10.) Tallboys

11.) Styles

12.) Nidd

13.) Resthaven

14.) Danemead

15.) 12a Great Ormond Street

Chapter 2 - Animals
pets, witnesses, accomplices..

1.) Although Roderick Alleyn prefers cats his mother breeds Alsatians. What is the name of her prize bitch?

2.) Which great-aunt of Tommy Beresford left her money to a home for cats?

3.) What is the name of Albert Campion's son's dog?

4.) What is the unusual hobby of Lord Peter Wimsey's friend and lawyer Sir Impey Biggs?

5.) Albert Campion gave his whippet "*..useless for detection..*" to the twins. What was that dog's name?

6.) To which cat did Roderick Alleyn say, "*..my good woman.. you've been eating fish..*"

7.) What are the physical peculiarities of Agatha Troy's cat?

8.) Bunch and Julian Harmon, friends of Miss Jane Marple, have a biblically-named cat called.. what?

9.) Samuel Whipplestone, a friend of Roderick Alleyn, has a cat called.. what?

10.) What kind of pet is Albert Campion's Autolycus?

11.) Agatha Troy encounters convicted killer *"Kittiwee the Cook"* and his two cats called.. what?

12.) What is the name of Albert Campion's white mouse?

13.) Amanda Fitton's Aunt Hatt has a fat shepherd-dog called.. what?

14.) Pronounced *"Foon"* what is the name of Marcus Featherstone's (friend of Albert Campion) dog?

15.) Which sleuth said *"..I am not.. obsessed with dogs. I, personally, can live without the dog.."* ?

16.) Who is the cat who *"..lives in two households and is owned by no one.."* encountered by Miss Maud Silver?

17.) When Albert Campion's friend Guffy Randall is told by a palmist that *"..a beautiful creature will throw him over.."* he refuses to ride his horse for two weeks. Then his fiancee ends their engagement. Who does he later marry?

18.) Hercule Poirot broke up a *"dog-napping"* ring which this woman, aided by her Pekinese, operated.. who was she?

19.) Who is the cat Miss Maud Silver saved from a gas-poisoning death?

20.) What are the names of Cicely Hathaway's, (Frank Abbott's cousin), two dogs?

21.) What animal did Lugg keep at Carrados Square?

22.) The Dowager Duchess of Denver, Lord Peter Wimsey's mother, has a cat called.. what?

Chapter 3 - Capital Punishment

identify the character based on his or her opinion of hanging

1.) "..I got permission to see a hanging once.. but it hasn't cured me of meddling..".

2.) "..it's nothing reasonable - nothing I can attempt to justify. It's simply that I've got an absolute horror of capital punishment. I don't even know if I agree with the stock arguments against it. It's just one of those nightmare things..".

3.) "..contrary to my usual reaction, I rather hope this chap will hang..".

4.) "..I am really very, very sorry.. that they have abolished capital punishment because I do feel that if there is anyone who ought to hang, it is..".

5.) "..if it takes me the rest of my life, and if it costs me my job, by God! If I have to do the killing myself, I'll get this murderer and see him suffer for it..".

6.) "..I neither like it nor dislike it.. once I've delivered the man to the court I reckon my business is done. I'm the dog. I bring in the bird. I don't expect to have to cook him..".

7.) *"..I have never regretted my part in bringing that man to justice. I've no patience with modern humanitarian scruples about capital punishment..".*

8.) *"..a murderer.. is more conceited than any creature on this earth.. therefore he (or she) goes ahead just the same, and all you can have is the satisfaction of hanging them afterwards..".*

Chapter 4 - Careers

skills, tools-of-the-trade, and famous cases from the past..

1.) Whose door has a brass plaque stating the sleuth's name and the words *"The Goods Dept."* ?

2.) Who has a malacca cane *"..marked off in inches.. concealing a sword in its belly and a compass in its head.."* ?

3.) Whose job is described *"..you're not a Private Eye and you're not an amateur. I expect we look on you as an Expert, a chap we call in.."* ?

4.) For what sleuthing purpose does Lord Peter Wimsey affect a monocle?

5.) Who said *"..I landed in Labrador from a friend's yacht once, and the man in the village store said: You wear your moustache shorter now, Sgt.."* ?

6.) Whose first case, in 1921, was called *"The Attenbury Emeralds"* ?

7.) Hercule Poirot was originally a policeman in Belgium. What rank had he achieved when he retired?

8.) Which sleuth says the purpose behind undertaking an investigation is "..*to find the truth and serve justice, not prove innocence or guilt..*" ?

9.) Who saved his brother's life by proving a murder accusation false?

10.) Who often refers to *"The Case of the Soap Manufacturer of Lieges"*, a man who poisoned his wife in order to marry his blonde secretary?

11.) Which sleuth's first case was *"The Urtingham Pearls"* ?

12.) Which sleuth claims to have "..*special gifts of observation..*", of "..*knowing human nature..*", of being "..*able to draw parallels from village life..*" ?

13.) Which sleuth commits a murder?

14.) Which sleuth determines criminals "..*by the look of their face..*" and has never lost a case?

15.) Which sleuth met his future wife at her murder trial?

16.) Which sleuth believes that women generally "..*do not appreciate the abstract passion for justice..*" ?

17.) Hercule Poirot once retired and planned to grow what in his garden?

18.) Which sleuth frequently refers to the intriguingly titled *"Case of the Poisoned Caterpillars"* ?

19.) Roderick Alleyn became *"..the youngest Chief Inspector in Scotland Yard history.."* at what age?

20.) Which sleuth's first case was *"The Crime at Black Dudley"* ?

21.) Who taught Miss Maud Silver how to shoot a pistol?

22.) Which sleuth turned down the Governorship of an island?

23.) Tommy and Tuppence Beresford run Blunt's Brilliant Detectives on behalf of the owner who is a friend of whom?

24.) Miss Jane Marple is able to solve the mystery of *"The Four Suspects"* because her German governess taught her what Victorian skill?

25.) Which sleuth served in the Diplomatic Corps from 1919-1920 and speaks conversational French and Italian?

Chapter 5 - Cars
The love affair with the automobile..

1.) What kind of car does Lugg acquire in later life?

2.) In what Ngaio Marsh novel would you find a local taxi called *"The Bloodbath"* ?

3.) Who owns a car they find very difficult to get out of?

4.) Who are the three sleuths who do not drive?

5.) What kind of car does Hercule Poirot own?

6.) At this sleuth's first appearance he can't afford to run a car but later acquires a Lagonda then a Bentley. Who is he?

7.) By what name does Lord Peter Wimsey call his Daimlers?

8.) Of which sleuth's car is it said *"..there's one gear..any other handle you pull you get your money back.."* ?

9.) What does Valentine Ferris (Albert Campion's sister) call her car?

10.) What is the name of the taxi-driver from Miss Jane Marple's village?

Chapter 6 – Clubs

"Waiter, take away Lord Whatsisname, he's been dead two days.." from a Punch cartoon

1.) What are the names of Albert Campion's three clubs?

2.) What are the names of Lord Peter Wimsey's three clubs?

3.) Whose club is *"The United Arts"* ?

Chapter 7 - Education

1.) Which sleuth's house at Oxford was *"Davidsons"*?

2.) As a child which sleuth attended *"Botolph's Abbey"*?

3.) Which sleuth's cousin is married to his school roommate and best friend?

4.) Which sleuth was taught by a German governess?

5.) Which sleuth was a governess for twenty years?

6.) In University which sleuth was nicknamed *"The Great Flim"*?

7.) Which sleuth went to *"St Agatha's, Oxford"* and *"St Ignatius College, Cambridge"*?

8.) Whose teacher was *"Old Miss Payne"*?

9.) Who *"..was taught knitting in the Continental manner by Fraulein Stein.."*?

10.) Which sleuth was sent to *"..a pensionnat in Florence.."*?

11.) Which sleuth took a First reading History at Balliol?

12.) Which sleuth studied at the Bar until a family dispute ended the funding of his legal career?

13.) Which sleuth claims the school motto of *"Floreat Fauna"* stood for *"grow, you little beasts"* ?

14.) Which sleuth enjoyed illicit after-hours feasts with schoolfriend Cecelia Voycey?

Chapter 8 - Family

"Give me a murder in quiet family surroundings, the kind you read about in the papers - not the explosive gangster type."
Agatha Christie

1.) What is Albert's true first name?

2.) Which of Maud Silver's nieces, Ethel and Gladys, is the elder?

3.) To which career does Ricky Alleyn aspire?

4.) Whose father died in the Crimean War?

5.) Who is Lord Peter Wimsey's ward?

6.) Whose daughter is called Hattie but *"..his wife preferred Atalanta.."* ?

7.) Jane's niece-in-law, Joan West, is aunt to whom?

8.) Albert's sister Valentine was disinherited for her marriage to Sidney Ferris. Who is her second husband?

9.) What was the married name of Lugg's sister?

10.) What are the names of the three children of Tommy and Tuppence Beresford?

11.) What was the maiden name of Roderick Alleyn's mother?

12.) What is the name of Albert and Amanda Campion's son?

13.) What is the name of Laura Rankin's, (cousin of Alan Grant), son?

14.) What are the names of Miss Maud Silver's parents?

15.) Who claims to be: "..a renegade Scot. My grandfather belonged to Strathspey.." ?

16.) Who is the niece of Roderick Alleyn involved in a murder during her Coming-Out season?

17.) In which book do we actually meet Sir George Alleyn?

Chapter 9 – Friends & Cohorts

"..and it said something for their friendship that neither of them felt the smallest embarrassment.." about Alleyn and Fox.

1.) In the Short Story *"The Blue Geranium"* Miss Jane Marple and Dolly Bantry are mere acquaintances, but by the time of which novel they are great friends?

2.) Miss Maud Silver's *"dearest friend"* was Mary Meredith. What is the name of Mary's daughter?

3.) What is the name of Albert Campion's American friend who teaches History?

4.) What are the names of the erudite vicar and his *"terrifying wife"* who are good friends of Miss Jane Marple?

5.) Which friend of Albert Campion's inherited a family business that includes the forging of antique jewelry?

6.) Rietta Cray and Randal March, (friends of Miss Maud Silver), eventually marry and raise a family. What are the names of their children?

7.) Who is Albert Campion's disreputable dancing-master friend *"..thin, elderly and affected.."* with a Studio in Cavendish Square?

8.) What newspaper does Lord Peter Wimsey's friend Salcombe Hardy work for?

9.) What is Colonel Race's, (friend to Hercule Poirot), Christian name?

10.) What are the names of Marta Hallard's parents?

11.) Who is Troy's best friend?

12.) What is the name of Roderick Alleyn's *"friendly newshound"* ?

13.) What is the name of the Police-Surgeon Roderick Alleyn always requests?

Chapter 10 – Habits

in response to readers' concerns over Miss Maud Silver's health Patricia Wentworth wrote: "..Her occasional slight cough is merely a means of self-expression. It does not indicate any bronchial infection..".

1.) Who has "..*a child's waterpistol fashioned to look like a revolver..*" ?

2.) Who has the "..*habit of moistening his forefinger when turning a page..*" ?

3.) Which two sleuths don't smoke?

4.) Who has "..*spiky, spidery handwriting heavily-underlined.. like a spider in an ink bottle..*" ?

5.) Who has distinctive handwriting "..*square with heavy downstrokes and sharp Greek Es..*" ?

6.) Who takes sugar, never saccharine, in coffee but only milk in tea?

7.) Who drinks hot chocolate instead of tea?

8.) Which sleuth claims "..*to have no truck with doctors and their medicines.. grandmother's tansy tea is equal to any amount of drugs..*" ?

9.) Who has a penchant for munching on apples?

10.) Who buys pyjamas from Dodds "..*altered to have a piece of flannel sewn across the shoulderblades..*"?

11.) Who smokes tiny Russian cigarettes?

12.) Who can't stand hearing foreign languages spoken?

13.) Who collects First Editions?

14.) Whose favourite colour is bright blue, and second favourite is pink?

15.) Who thinks a square egg would be ideal?

16.) Who only reads the Obituaries section of The Times?

17.) Which sleuth "..*sends the plate and the King Charles tankard to the bank and puts the maid on board-wages..*" while away?

18.) Who wears only black patent-leather shoes - even in the country?

19.) Whose tailor is Jamieson & Fellowes?

20.) Which sleuth is a lifelong avid gardener?

21.) What is Miss Maud Silver's nightly bedtime reading?

Chapter 11 – Matchmaking

*"As I grow older and older
And totter towards the tomb,
I find that I care less and less
Who goes to bed with whom"*
Dorothy L. Sayers

Agatha Troy	Alan Dell
Amanda Fitton	Albert Campion
Angela North	Andrew Bantling
Bridget Paget	Arthur Hastings
Cicely Abbott	Augustus Randall
Dulcibella Duveen	Charles Luke
Harriet Vane	Charles Moray
Henrietta Cray	Charles Parker
Isobel Lobbett	Frederick Arbuthnot
Janet Pursuivant	Gilbert Whippet
Joan/Joyce Lempriere	Giles Paget
Margaret Langton	Grant Hathaway
Mary Fitton	Marlowe Lobbett
Mary Wimsey	Nigel Bathgate
Nicola Maitland-Mayne	Peter Wimsey
Prudence Cowley	Randall March
Rachel Levy	Raymond West
Valentine Ferris	Roderick Alleyn
Victoria Prunella Scroop-Dory	Thomas Beresford

Chapter 12 – Nicknames & Aliases

"As it emerges today the detective story proper is a form of entertainment almost entirely cerebral, since it aims to provide a means of escape for those who do not wish, for some excellent private reason, to take their emotions for a ride. .the puzzle is the thing." Margery Allingham

1.) P.E. Garbel, a relation of Agatha Troy's, calls Troy and Rory... what?

2.) Who is known as *"Pickled Gherkin"*?

3.) What friend of Roderick Alleyn's is nicknamed *"Bunchy"* ?

4.) Who calls Albert Campion *"..Orph.. short for Orpheus as in Orpheus and his Lute.."* ?

5.) Who is called *"Cid"* by his son?

6.) Captain Arthur Hastings calls his wife *"Cinderella"*, what is her real name?

7.) Who is called *"Uncle Beastly"* ?

8.) Who is Roderick Alleyn's schoolmate nicknamed *"The Boomer"* ?

9.) Who named his beard *"..impudence, persuasion out of cheek.."* ?

10.) Who is *"Miss Robinson"* ?

11.) Who is the English crook called *"The Destroyer"* detected by Hercule Poirot?

12.) Who calls Miss Jane Marple *"Nemesis"* ?

13.) What is Albert Campion's Christian name?

14.) Who is C.J. Broderick?

15.) What do Albert Campion and friends call the elderly Lady Larradine?

16.) Whose surname is translated as *"Vainse"*

17.) Mrs Sarah, matriarch of the Gypsies, calls Albert Campion... what?

18.) Who is Death Bredon?

19.) Who do the newspapers call *"The Handsome Sleuth"* ?

20.) Who is *"Maggers"* ?

21.) Who is *"Birdie"* ?

22.) Who is *"Polly"* ?

23.) Who is *"Lalla"* ?

24.) Who is *"Br'er Fox"*?

25.) What shortening of his name does Albert Campion detest?

26.) Fill in the blanks on these AKAs of Albert Campion:
    Christopher _____
    Mr _____ Dodd
    The Hon. _____ Ash
    Albert _____
    _____ Booth

27.) What is the real name of Tuppence Beresford?

28.) Who is Septimus Falls?

29.) Who is Patricia Blenkensop?

Chapter 13 – Old Tragedies

1.) Which book refers to the Opera "Lucia di Lammermoor" ?

2.) Which book refers to the Play *"The Duchess of Malfi"* ?

3.) Which book tells of Sandra Compline who had a wax face-lift by Franz Hartz to regain her straying husband but the surgery didn't take and the result was disastrous?

4.) Which book tells of Hal Huntingforest marrying Mary Fitton the day before he left for the Crimean War where he was killed but Mary's mother-in-law, Josephine, forces the young Vicar to destroy the marriage record?

5.) Which book tells the story that during the war Ludovic Danberry-Phinn, private secretary to Sir Harold Lackland, is wrongly accused of treason and commits suicide?

6.) Which books tells of James Barton, badly wounded in the Far East, returning home from war to find his wife living with another man and when he killed them both being sent to the Asylum for the Criminally Insane at Broadmoor?

7.) Which book tells the tale of a vendetta between the Pepitone and Rossi families where only women are killed, beginning with "*..the murder of a Pepitone girl by her Rossi bridegroom..*"?

Chapter 14 – Personal Staff

Albert Campion to his manservant Lugg: "..I want my things packed for a week and yours too. Not in the same bag.."

1.) What is the name of Roderick Alleyn's manservant?

2.) Who was his previous employer?

3.) What is the name of the boy-turned-manservant of Tommy and Tuppence Beresford?

4.) What was his previous employment?

5.) What is the full name of Albert Campion's manservant?

6.) What was his previous employment?

7.) What is the full name of Lord Peter Wimsey's manservant?

8.) Who was his previous employer?

9.) Name Alan Grant's daily?

10.) What was her previous employment?

11.) Who was the *"Domestic Engineer"* Raymond West hired after Miss Jane Marple's bout with pneumonia?

12.) What is the surname of Miss Jane Marple's *"Faithful Florence"* ?

13.) What are the two names (due to an editing error) by which Miss Maud Silver's housekeeper is called?

14.) What is the name of Albert Campion's family chauffeur?

15.) Who is Mr Satterthwaite's chauffeur?

16.) What does Hercule Poirot call his manservant?

17.) Tommy and Tuppence Beresford's manservant eventually grows up, marries Amy and they open a pub. What are the names of their three children?

18.) What was Lugg's post during WWII?

19.) Cherry and Jim Baker originally came from Huddersfield. Before they moved in with Miss Jane Marple they lived at what address in *"The Development"* ?

20.) Who is Bunter's *"..only relative.."* ?

21.) Except in a different novel we learn that Bunter is one of.. how many?

22.) How old was Albert Campion when he acquired Lugg?

23.) Hercule Poirot's secretary, Miss Lemon, dreams of developing the perfect.. what?

24.) What is the name of Alan Grant's landlady?

Chapter 15 – Personal Trivia

1.) Who "..looks like a cross between a monk and a grandee - more grandee in evening clothes.." ?

2.) Who has a penchant for buying hats?

3.) Who was born on May 20th, 1900?

4.) who has "..according to co-workers, only two weaknesses 'coffee and coffee'.." ?

5.) Who maintains *"..a bank balance of 444 pounds, 4 shillings and 4 pence.."* ?

6.) Who *"..runs in an odd, hen-like manner.."* ?

7.) Whose phone number is 395?

8.) Who was born in 1896?

9.) Who has twins born in 1929?

10.) Whose birthday is August 4th?

11.) Who is constantly redesigning her hair into elaborate styles?

12.) Who based his new career on information learned during 35 years as a civil servant?

13.) Who "..*looks like an athletic don with a hint of the Army somewhere..*"

14.) Alan Grant claims his palate is his "..*most precious possession..*" and, as a result, never eats.. what?

15.) Who was called "..*a cross between a bear and a baby and exhibited the most pleasing traits of both creatures..*" ?

16.) Who always travels with a pair of curling tongs?

17.) Who has "..*brown, slightly protuberant eyes like large peppermint bulleyes..*" ?

18.) Hercule Poirot and Mr Satterthwaite share what common malady?

19.) Who wears pince-nez for "..*occasional use for very fine print..*" ?

20.) Who is Albert Campion's Doctor?

21.) Who is Lord Peter Wimsey's Doctor?

22.) Which sleuth suffers from claustrophobia?

Chapter 16 – Policemen

"Death, in particular, seems to provide the mind of the Anglo-Saxon race with a greater fund of innocent amusement than any other single subject." Dorothy L. Sayers

1.) Which policeman has *"..a face carved out of wood.."* ?

2.) What is Superintendent Yeo's Christian name?

3.) Who is Superintendent Battle's policeman nephew?

4.) Who is Sir Henry Clithering's policeman godson?

5.) What is Chief-Superintendent Oates Christian name?

6.) Who is Chief-Superintendent Oates secretary?

7.) Which policeman spends years learning French from home study courses?

8.) This policeman's youngest (of five) children was accused of theft by Miss Amphrey, headmistress of Meadway.

9.) Identify Chief-Inspector Ernest Lamb's three daughters.

10.) Which policeman has "..*gray cold eyes as bleak as the North Sea..*"?

11.) Which policeman's hangout is "..*the Coach and Horses pub at the wrong end of Early Street..*"?

12.) What is the name of Chief-Superintendent Oates wife?

13.) Whose pet phrase is "..*we'll have to get you into the force..*"?

14.) Who is Alan Grant's boss?

15.) Alan Grant's sergeant, Williams, is married to Nora. Name their two children.

16.) Due to his contempt for "..*fancy-dress coppers..*" which policeman's only disguise is "..*an ancient Donegal tweed ulster and an out-of-date felt hat..*" which makes him look like "..*a North of Ireland corn chandler on holiday..*"?

17.) In what book does Albert Campion meet Inspector Charlie Luke?

18.) At the age of 43 he is "..*the youngest chief-inspector at the Central Branch of New Scotland Yard..*"

19.) What is the full name of Inspector Fox?

Chapter 17 – Publications
who wrote what?
(the author isn't necessarily a sleuth..)

1.) *"Notes for Collectors of Incunabula"*.

2.) *"The Body in the Library"* (NOT the Agatha Christie version).

3.) *"Principles and Practise of Criminal Investigation"*.

4.) *"Death in the Pot"*.

5.) *"The Affair of the Second Goldfish"*.

6.) Who wanted to write *"The Mystery of the Second Cucumber"* ?

7.) *"The History of Bells at Fenchurch St. Paul"*.

8.) *"The Duchess of Malfi"*.

9.) *"The Murderer's Compendium"*.

10.) *"Crabbed Age and Youth"*.

11.) *"Angelo in August"*.

12.) *"Simon in Latium"*.

13.) *"The Death in the Drainpipe"*.

14.) *"Memoirs of an Old Buffer"*.
15.) Who are Roderick Alleyn's publishers?

16.) Whose fictional sleuth is called *"Sven Hjerson"* ?

17.) Whose fictional sleuth is called *"Robert Templeton"* ?

18.) What's the name of the local newspaper at Gyrth and Pontisbright?

19.) What's the name of the local newspaper at St Mary Mead?

20.) What's the name of the local newspaper at Chipping Cleghorn?

21.) The play *"Little Mary"* made Miss Jane Marple and Colonel Easterly blush. Who wrote it?

22.) Who is the author behind pen name Aubrey Mandrake?

23.) Which novelist and noted poet writes without capital letters?

24.) What old book does Lord Peter Wimsey's nephew, Jerry, buy which contains a map of buried treasure?

25.) Who claims to have written *"Character from Characters, or How to Tell Your Lover by his Note"* ?

26.) Who writes a newspaper column called *"..The Helping Hand.. ask G.P.F. (Guide, Philosopher, Friend) about it.."* ?

27.) Who promises Albert Campion *"..an illuminated address of 5,000 words, written in my own hand, and coloured.."* if Albert catches a society blackmailer?

28.) Who is writing the novel *"Elephants do Forget"* ?

29.) Harriet Vane was able to afford her wedding gift to Lord Peter Wimsey by writing a 3,500 word short story for what publication?

30.) Who wrote *"Under the Fig Tree"* and is currently writing *"Snow on the Desert's Face"* ?

31.) Who said, of detective novelists, *"..he heads one chapter 'Routine', dismisses six weeks of drudgery in as many phrases, cuts the cackle and gets to the 'osses. I wish to the Lord we could follow his lead.."* ?

32.) Who wrote *"The Scaly Breed"* ?

33.) Which Lethal Lady wrote *"Unpopular Opinions"* ?

34.) Which Lethal Lady's autobiography is called *"Come, Tell Me How You Live"* ?

35.) Which Lethal Lady's autobiography is called *"Black Beech and Honeydew"* ?

Chapter 18 – Quotes

Part 1 - identify the sleuth from these very characteristic quotes..

1.) "..inexperienced young women are sadly liable to be carried away by specious arguments on the subject of free union and companionate marriage. They fail to realize until too late that though civilized marriage laws may sometimes prove irksome, they nevertheless exist for the protection of women and family.."

2.) "..it casts a spurious but acceptable glamour over the more squalid aspects of my profession.."

3.) "..when I know what the murderer is like, I shall be able to find out who he is.."

4.) "..if anyone over the age of sixty-five finds fault with you never argue. Never try to say you're right. Apologize at once and say it was all your fault and you're very sorry and you'll never do it again.."

5.) "..I always believe the worst. What is so sad is that one is usually justified in doing so.."

6.) "..would it invite confidence more, d'you suppose, if I dyed my hair black an' grew a Newgate fringe? It's very tryin', you can't think, always to look as if one's name was Algy.."

Part 2 - identify the sleuth from the words of another..

7.) "..as far as.. was concerned the human race was glass-fronted, and, furthermore that.. saw right past the shop-window into the back premises.."

8.) "..he was, I might almost say, exceptionally ordinary-looking.. sleek, pale hair, and one of those rather stupid faces with a long nose and monocle.."

9.) When asked if he'd heard of "*The Rape of Lucrece*" replied: "I can't say I have unless it's on the police list which it sounds as if it might be. Or would it be Shakespeare?"

10.) "..last time I saw him we walked down Regent Street together, and from the corner of Conduit Street to the Circus we met five people he knew, including a Viscountess and two Bishops. Each of them stopped and greeted him as an old pal and every single one of them called him by a different name.."

11.) "..is just the finest detective God ever made. Natural genius cultivated in a suitable soil.."

12.) "..a dark handsome deeply bronzed man of fifty, he was usually to be found in some outpost of the Empire - especially if there were trouble brewing.."

13.) *"..you don't even have to say: 'Hop it!' You just look at them, and they begin to recollect appointments.."*

Chapter 19 – Religion

"..with the devoted acquiescence of a good Catholic although, of course theistically, she professes the mysteries of Old Nile.." Octavius Danberry-Phinn on Mrs Thomasina Twitchett

1.) Which sleuth "..not for the first time felt his own lack of acceptance to be tinged with a faint regret.."?

2.) Which sleuth is one of a Country Vicar's five daughters?

3.) Whose mother belongs to the Church Militant?

4.) Who considers fishing "..a cross between a sport and a religion.."?

5.) Who lives next door to a Vicarage?

6.) Whose Victoria tea-set is missing one cup "..broken by Great-Aunt Louisa's Vicar when he slammed it into its saucer to emphasize his point that Eve's sin forced subjugation on all women.."?

7.) Whose uncle was the Bishop of Ely?

8.) Whose uncle was Canon of St. Peter the Gate?

9.) Whose godfather was the Bishop of Devizes?

10.) Whose uncle was the Canon of Chichester Cathedral?

11.) Who is a Catholic who "..*strongly believes in the force of superstition..*"?

12.) The text *"Ask And Ye Shall Receive"* was pinned over whose childhood bed?

13.) A modern painting of a Madonna and Child seemed to which sleuth's "..*simple, evangelical mind.. an abominable blasphemy..*"?

14.) Who reads a portion of Scripture every night?

15.) What is the name of the Church at Duke's Denver?

Chapter 20 – Romance

"When Sayers fell in love with her creation she made quite an ass out of both of them"
Ngaio Marsh

1.) Who married someone else because she thought Albert Campion was *"..comic about women.."* ?

2.) Which confirmed bachelor almost proposed when in Kew Gardens *"..to see the bluebells.."* ?

3.) Whose mother hoped her son would marry Evelyn Curtis, daughter of her greatest friend?

4.) Who keeps photo mementos of the couples brought together as a result of successful sleuthing?

5.) What was Troy painting when she met Roderick?

6.) Albert Campion keeps *"..a small, yellow-flowered button from her dress.."* .. whose?

7.) What was the name of Lord Peter Wimsey's first fiancee?

8.) Who calls Albert Campion *"The Universal Aunt"* ?

9.) Alan Grant met which woman when her pearls were stolen?

10.) Who was Harriet Vane's live-in lover?

11.) Whose fiance was murdered and her brother charged with the crime?

12.) Whose Aunt Primrose "..had been in and out of 11 Nursing Homes.." before falling in love with the much-younger Mervyn and planned to set up house with him in Aberdeen until he was arrested?

13.) Who was the Best Man at Harriet and Peter's wedding?

14.) Whose daughter was Lugg once engaged to?

15.) With what words does Troy accept Roderick Alleyn's proposal?

16.) What words did Peter Wimsey say when he proposed, and was accepted, by Harriet Vane?

Chapter 21 – Scotland Yard

"Now if a woman were the head of Scotland Yard.." Ariadne Oliver

1.) Who is *"..Father Superior of the second most tough police division in Metro London and proud of it.."* ?

2.) Who is godfather to Chief-Superintendent Oates son?

3.) Who has Room 49 at the Yard?

4.) When asked if he's *"..the star turn at Scotland Yard.."* who replies: *"..oh no.. I come in bundles.."* ?

5.) When Roderick Alleyn calls for *"Flash and Dabs"* (Photographer and Fingerprinter), who does he get?

6.) What is the phone number of New Scotland Yard?

Chapter 22 – Sherlock Holmes
"..old Conan Doyle knew his job.."
Roderick Alleyn

1.) Who said *"..I think part of the charm of those excellent tales lies in Watson's casual but enthralling references to cases we never hear of again.."* ?

2.) Who does the Daily Mirror call *"The Sherlock Holmes of the West End"* ?

3.) Who said *"..I'm an old-fashioned woman and I call it mother-wit, and it's so rare for a man to have it that if he does you write a book about him and call him Sherlock Holmes.."* ?

4.) Sergeant Williams, at the age of eleven, hid *"..in a hayloft in Worchestershire trying to read _____ without being discovered by Authority, who had banned it.."* What Sherlock Holmes story was he reading?

Chapter 23 – Sports & Games
identify the book

1.) Cricket

2.) Fishing (two books)

3.) Gymnastics

4.) Tennis

5.) Bridge

6.) Mah Jongg

7.) Golf

8.) The Murder Game (three books)

9.) A Darts game of Round-the-Clock

Chapter 24 – St Mary Mead

"Living in St Mary Mead does give one an insight into human nature." Jane Marple

1.) What is the County?

2.) What is the Shire?

3.) Where is the closest Train Station?

4.) What are the names of the four Taxi Companies?

5.) What are the names of the two Doctors?

6.) What is the name of the local Manor?

7.) What is the name of the local Orphanage?

8.) What is the name of the local Inn?

9.) Who is the Coroner?

10.) What is the name of the local Bank?

11.) Who is the Oldest Inhabitant?

12.) Who is the Gardener?

13.) Who is the Grocer?

14.) What is the name of the new suburb?

15.) What is the name of the Constable?

16.) What are the names of the two Inspectors?

17.) Who is the Chief Constable?

18.) What is the name of the Curate?

Chapter 25 – Trivial Trivia

answers to these general questions are found in the novels and short stories..

1.) What direction is *"widdershins"* ?

2.) *"Dactylography"* is the study of what?

3.) Who wrote *"The Bride of Lammermoor"* ?

4.) Which French gentleman invented the *"Portrait Parle"* and the *"Fingerprint Theory"* ?

5.) Which peer created the Police College?

6.) What is the name of the Police College?

7.) In what textbook would you find:
*What was the crime? Who did it?
When was it done? and Where?
How done? and with what motive?
Who on the deed did share?*

8.) Every English county has a Criminal Investigation Division (C.I.D). If they call in Scotland Yard who pays the investigation cost?

9.) What are *"Hudson's Processes"* ?

10.) In Miss Jane Marple's time what did the word banting mean?

11.) In what book would one find the litany:

*From Envy, Hatred, Malice
and all Uncharitableness
Good Lord deliver us*

12.) What was the name of the Times critic and crossword puzzler constructor during the war years? and who was his successor?

13.) In the Vehicle Registry the name listed on the documents is called what?

14.) In Alan Grant's time it was illegal for stores to sell this after 9:00 pm.

15.) Crime Writers formed *"The Detective Club"* in 1932. Which of the Lethal Ladies was its second president, holding the office for nine years?

16.) Who and what was the club mascot?

17.) Translate the following Latin:
    Quomodo Quando Quibis Auxillis

18.) Debretts, Burkes and Landed Gentry are the Who's Who of the British Aristocracy. What is the Continental version called?

19.) What is a *"campion"* ?

20.) What is the English word for the French word *"chantage"* ?

21.) English Policeman cannot drink or.. what? while on duty?

22.) The *"Ingolldsby Legends"* tell the tale of the *"Hand of Glory"* (from the *"Compendium Maleficonum"*). What is it?

23.) What do the initials V.A.D represent?

24.) Name the Artist who painted the covers of Agatha Christie's books.

25.) Legal Aid available to the British needy is called what?

26.) This Latin phrase *"Quis, Quid, Ubi, Quius Auxiliis, Cur, Quomondo, Quando"* is known as the what?

27.) To what are the stories referring when they use the word receipt?

28.) What are the Seven Deadly Sins?

29.) What are the Seven Virtues?

Chapter 26 – Unusual Weapons
identify the book..

1.) Blunt Instrument: a jeroboam of champagne.

2.) Deadly spray in a nasal inhaler.

3.) A Russian dagger used during a game of Murder.

4.) A ceremonial African spear.

5.) A gun placed inside a piano and hooked to the soft pedal.

6.) A silver-plated skewer through the eye.

7.) A Chinese dagger once owned by Marco Polo.

8.) Cyanide in the stem of a pipe.

9.) Weed-killer in a perfume atomizer.

Chapter 27 – Wartime

"You've become an epicure of violence which is as much as to say a 'bloody snob'" Roderick Alleyn

1.) Who attained the rank of Major in WWI?

2.) During WWI Albert Campion was in the Afghanistan Campaign. How long did he serve?

3.) Why did Frank Abbott have four applications to the RAF rejected?

4.) During WWII a bomb exploded on Miss Maud Silver's street. What damage was done to her apartment?

5.) After being wounded on the Belgian Front in WWI who was invalided out to serve as a Recruiting Officer?

6.) From which branch of the forces was Chief Inspector Lamb refused in WWI?

7.) Who was Tommy Beresford's superior, nicknamed *"Old Josh"* ?

8.) Who suffered a breakdown lasting two years after being buried in *"..a shell-hole at Caudry.."* ?

9.) Where was Albert Campion during WWII?

10.) Who was "..trapped in the Antipodes.. tracking Fifth Columnists?

11.) What was Tommy Beresford's rank in WWI?

12.) What war work did Troy perform for the Army?

13.) What did Amanda Campion refer to as her *"war work"* ?

14.) What was the name of the General Tuppence Beresford drove during WWI?

15.) What was the name of the Boarding-House where Tuppence Beresford posed as a twice-married woman with three sons?

16.) Who is the subject of this quote: *"..He belonged to a post-war generation, that particular generation which was too young for one war and most prematurely too old for the next.. His was the age which had never known illusion, the grimly humourous generation which from childhood had both expected and experienced the seamier side.."* ?

17.) Who spent *"..four years on the Western Front.."* ?

18.) Who was Troy painting when Roderick Alleyn returned home?

Chapter 28 – Wills & Epitaphs
Here Lie I, Poor Albert Campion
Death was Bad, but Life - was Champion

1.) Roderick Alleyn's French Teacher, Miss Emily Pride, inherited.. what? from her sister Fanny Bottom?

2.) Who was the sole beneficiary of a fortune because *"..she is too young to be mercenary.."* ?

3.) Who left Miss Jane Marple a legacy of 20,000 pounds sterling if she would fulfill a commission?

4.) From whom did Miss Maud Silver inherit her carved bog-oak rose brooch?

5.) The Bishop of Devizes received a precious gift from his old flame Elise de Bragelonne which he, in turned, bequeathed to Albert Campion. What was it?

6.) In which novel does Miss Maud Silver assist an heiress obligated to make an annual will?

7.) Lord Peter Wimsey helps Hannah Marryat find the will for a 250,000 pound sterling estate. Where had her uncle hidden the clue?

8.) After having known Lady Amanda Fitton for one week Albert Campion named her beneficiary on his insurance policy. For how much?

9.) Lord Peter Wimsey claims to be writing a book about interesting wills entitled what?

10.) Great-Uncle Joseph Ferguson (a suicide at age 95) bequeathed.. what? to his Medical Student nephew Thomas MacPherson?

Chapter 29 – About the Authors

"I just slid into detective writing.. I had no notion I should be wedded to it for the rest of my life." Ngaio Marsh

1.) She was born.. when?

    1.) 1890
    2.) 1893
    3.) 1899
    4.) 1904
    5.) 1878
    6.) 1896

2.) She was born.. where?

    1.) Christchurch, New Zealand
    2.) Torquay, England
    3.) Scotland
    4.) East Anglia, England
    5.) Mussoorie, India

3.) Who is she *Also Known As* ?

    1.) Elizabeth McIntosh
    2.) Mrs Max Mallowan
    3.) Edith
    4.) Mrs Fleming
    5.) Dora Amy Elles Dillon Turnbull
    6.) Mrs Phillip Youngman Carter
    7.) Mary Westmacott
    8.) Gordon Daviot
    9.) Maxwell March

4.) Small Scandals.. who?

　　1.) Her second husband was 20 years her junior.

　　2.) She bore an illegitimate son.

　　3.) When located, after several days disappearance, who was registered in a hotel using the name of her husband's mistress.

5.) Her First Whodunit.. was?

　　1.) A Man Lay Dead
　　2.) The White Cottage Mystery
　　3.) The Astonishing Adventure of Jane Smith
　　4.) The Corpse in the Bathtub
　　5.) The Mysterious Affair at Styles

6.) Her Last Whodunit.. was?

　　1.) Light Thickens
　　2.) A Cargo of Eagles
　　3.) Elephants can Remember

7.) She worked as a.. what?

　　1.) Hospital Dispensary Clerk
　　2.) Actress
　　3.) Film Production
　　4.) Theatre Producer
　　5.) Trainee Opera Singer
　　6.) Historic Writer

7.) Religious Writer
8.) Travel Writer
9.) Advertising Copywriter
10.) Landscape Painter

8.) She was awarded.. what?

1.) M.A. at Somerville College, Oxford, reading History.
2.) Her "damery" for her work in the revival of live theatre at her birthplace.
3.) In 1956 the "Order of the British Empire".

9.) She died.. when?

1.) 1952
2.) 1957
3.) 1961
4.) 1966
5.) 1976
6.) 1982

10.) Tough Stuff

1.) She was killed in a car crash.

2.) Her father was an American.

3.) From what language does the name "Ngaio" come?

4.) How many times was "The Mysterious Affair at Styles" rejected before Agatha Christie found a publisher?

5.) Margery Allingham's first novel (published in book form in 1974) was serialized in what newspaper?

6.) For what special occasion was Agatha Christie asked to write a radio play?

7.) In "Death and the Dancing Footman" Ngaio Marsh refers to another Lethal Lady, mentioning that writer's book. Which author, and what book?

8.) In "The Body in the Library" Agatha Christie refers to another Lethal Lady when one of her characters claims to have the writer's autograph. Which writer?

9.) What is Agatha Christie's full name, including maiden and married names?

10.) In 1929 Dorothy Sayers put together the first major Mystery Anthology. What was it called?

11.) Whose hobby was motorcycling?

Chapter 30 – The Really Tough Trivia
Good Luck!

1.) What is Albert Campion's S.S.#?

2.) In what magazine was Roderick Alleyn's home featured?

3.) Whose phone number is 395?

4.) Whose phone number is Regent 01300?

5.) Whose phone number is Norwood 4380?

6.) Whose phone number is Sloane 84405?

7.) Whose phone number is 21 Lenfold?

8.) Who likes *"..weak tea with three drops of milk.."* ?

9.) What is Roderick Alleyn's favourite flower?

10.) What annual Christmas present does Alan Grant give his daily?

11.) Who speaks French *"..in the honourable tradition of the Prioress in the Canterbury Tales.."* ?

12.) Who likes a $3^{3/4}$ minute egg?

13.) What is Albert Campion's shoe size?

14.) Where, in Suva, does George Alleyn live?

15.) Where did Tuppence and Tommy Beresford honeymoon?

16.) Who is Jane Marple's favourite painter?

17.) What is Roderick Alleyn's morning paper?

18.) Who are Albert Campion's brokers?

19.) When Tuppence worked in the hospital during WWI what were her bed rows?

20.) Who does Lugg call "..*The Prince of Parkhurst..*" ?

21.) What did Albert Campion store in Theo Bush's Museum of Wine?

22.) Name the 85-to-1 winner of the St Leger in Doncaster.

23.) Where does Inspector Fox go for his annual holiday?

24.) Agatha Christie brought Hercule Poirot to the stage in what play?

Chapter 31 – Fun With Book Titles

Numbers Game - List all (or any) of the books with the following numbers in their title:
1.) 0
2.) 1
3.) 2
4.) 3
5.) 4
6.) 5
7.) 6
8.) 7
9.) 8
10.) 9
11.) 10

Colour Scheme - List all (or any) of the books with the following colours in their title:
12.) Black
13.) White
14.) Ivory
15.) Brown
16.) Gray or Grey
17.) Blue
18.) Red
19.) Green

Where in the World? Identify the place in the title:

    20.) 4:50 from _____

    21.) Murder on the _____ Coach

    22.) Murder on the _____ Express

    23.) The Tiger in the _____

    24.) Passenger to _____

    25.) They Came to _____

    26.) Death on the _____

Who said that? Identify the <u>source of the quotation</u> in the title:

    27.) The Moving Finger

    28.) The Mirror Crack'd from Side to Side

    29.) The Labours of Hercules

    30.) The Singing Sands

    31.) By the Pricking of my Thumbs

    32.) The Pale Horse

    33.) There is a Tide

    34.) Sad Cypress

    35.) Postern of Fate

    36.) More Work for the Undertaker

Chapter 32 – Novels *"Also Known As"*
You eagerly snatch up a mystery at the Used Bookstore thinking "Hey! I've never read this one!" only to discover it's been published under another name..

1.) Alibi

2.) And Then There Were None

3.) Anna, Where Are You?

4.) An Overdose Of Death

5.) A Surfeit Of Lampreys

6.) A Wreath For Rivera

7.) Blood Will Tell

8.) The Boomerang Clue

9.) Brat Farrar

10.) The Bride of Death

11.) Come And Be Hanged

12.) Coroner's Pidgin

13.) The Corpse In The Bathtub

14.) Dancers in Mourning

15.) Danger Point

16.) Dark Threat

17.) The Dawson Pedigree

18.) Deadly Duo

19.) Death Of A Fool

20.) Destination Unknown
21.) Dumb Witness
22.) Eyewitness To Murder
23.) The Fear Sign
24.) Five Little Pigs
25.) Five Red Herrings
26.) Flowers for the Judge
27.) The Gazebo
28.) Gyrth Chalice Mystery
29.) Hercule Poirot's Christmas
30.) Hide My Eyes
31.) The Hollow
32.) Killer in the Crowd
33.) Lord Edgeware Dies
34.) The Mousetrap
35.) Murder After Hours
36.) Murder At Hazelmoor
37.) Murder in the Calais Coach
38.) Night At The Vulcan
39.) Out of the Past
40.) Remembered Death
41.) The Sabotage Murder Mystery
42.) Spotlight

43.) Taken At The Flood
44.) The Thirteen Problems

ANSWERS
Chapter 1 - Addresses

1.) 48 Regency Close
   Roderick Alleyn
2.) 15 Montague Mansions
   Maud Silver
3.) 100 Doughty Street
   Harriet Vane
4.) Duke's Denver
   Peter Wimsey's family home
5.) 12a Bottle Street
   Albert Campion
6.) Tatler's End
   Agatha Troy
7.) West Leaham Street
   Maud Silver
8.) 110a Piccadilly West
   Peter Wimsey
9.) Pontisbright Mill
   Amanda Fitton
10.) Tallboys
   Peter and Harriet Wimsey
11.) Styles
   Hercule Poirot
12.) Nidd
   Albert and Amanda Campion
13.) Resthaven
   Hercule Poirot
14.) Danemead
   Jane Marple
15.) 12a Great Ormond Street
   Charles Parker

ANSWERS
Chapter 2 – Animals

1.) Although Roderick Alleyn prefers cats his mother breeds Alsatians. What is the name of her prize bitch?
   Tunbridge Tessa
2.) Which great-aunt of Tommy Beresford left her money to a home for cats?
   Ada Fanshawe
3.) What is the name of Albert Campion's son's dog?
   Good-Dog Tray
4.) What is the unusual hobby of Lord Peter Wimsey's friend and lawyer Sir Impey Biggs?
   Raising prize-winning canaries
5.) Albert Campion gave his whippet *"..useless for detection.."* to the twins. What was that dog's name?
   Addlepate
6.) To which cat did Roderick Alleyn say, *"..my good woman.. you've been eating fish.."*
   Mrs Thomasina Twitchett
7.) What are the physical peculiarities of Agatha Troy's cat?
   it has three legs and one eye
8.) Bunch and Julian Harmon, friends of Miss Jane Marple, have a biblically-named cat called.. what?
   Tiglath Pilesar
9.) Samuel Whipplestone, a friend of Roderick Alleyn, has a cat called.. what?
   Lucy Lockett

10.) What kind of pet is Albert Campion's Autolycus?
- **a jackdaw**

11.) Agatha Troy encounters convicted killer *"Kittiwee the Cook"* and his two cats called.. what?
- **Smartypants and Slyboots**

12.) What is the name of Albert Campion's white mouse?
- **Haig**

13.) Amanda Fitton's Aunt Hatt has a fat shepherd-dog called.. what?
- **Choc-Ice**

14.) Pronounced *"Foon"* what is the name of Marcus Featherstone's (friend of Albert Campion) dog?
- **Featherstone Waugh**

15.) Which sleuth said *"..I am not.. obsessed with dogs. I, personally, can live without the dog.."* ?
- **Hercule Poirot**

16.) Who is the cat who *"..lives in two households and is owned by no one.."* encountered by Miss Maud Silver?
- **MacTavish**

17.) When Albert Campion's friend Guffy Randall is told by a palmist that *"..a beautiful creature will throw him over.."* he refuses to ride his horse for two weeks. Then his fiancee ends their engagement. Who does he later marry?
- **Mary Fitton**

18.) Hercule Poirot broke up a *"dog-napping"* ring which this woman, aided by her Pekinese, operated.. who was she?
Miss Amy Carnaby
19.) Who is the cat Miss Maud Silver saved from a gas-poisoning death?
Ablimech
20.) What are the names of Cicely Hathaway's, (Frank Abbott's cousin), two dogs?
Bramble and Tumble
21.) What animal did Lugg keep at Carrados Square?
a pig
22.) The Dowager Duchess of Denver, Lord Peter Wimsey's mother, has a cat called.. what?
Ahaseurus

ANSWERS
Chapter 3 - Capital Punishment

1.) "..I got permission to see a hanging once.. but it hasn't cured me of meddling..".
   Peter Wimsey

2.) "..it's nothing reasonable - nothing I can attempt to justify. It's simply that I've got an absolute horror of capital punishment. I don't even know if I agree with the stock arguments against it. It's just one of those nightmare things..".
   Troy

3.) "..contrary to my usual reaction, I rather hope this chap will hang..".
   Albert Campion

4.) "..I am really very, very sorry.. that they have abolished capital punishment because I do feel that if there is anyone who ought to hang, it is..".
   Jane Marple

5.) "..if it takes me the rest of my life, and if it costs me my job, by God! If I have to do the killing myself, I'll get this murderer and see him suffer for it..".
   Roderick Alleyn

6.) "..I neither like it nor dislike it.. once I've delivered the man to the court I reckon my business is done. I'm the dog. I bring in the bird. I don't expect to have to cook him..".
   Charlie Luke

7.) *"..I have never regretted my part in bringing that man to justice. I've no patience with modern humanitarian scruples about capital punishment..".*
   Jane Marple

8.) *"..a murderer.. is more conceited than any creature on this earth.. therefore he (or she) goes ahead just the same, and all you can have is the satisfaction of hanging them afterwards..".*
   Hercule Poirot

ANSWERS
Chapter 4 - Careers

1.) Whose door has a brass plaque stating the sleuth's name and the words *"The Goods Dept."* ?
   Albert Campion

2.) Who has a malacca cane *"..marked off in inches.. concealing a sword in its belly and a compass in its head.."* ?
   Peter Wimsey

3.) Whose job is described *"..you're not a Private Eye and you're not an amateur. I expect we look on you as an Expert, a chap we call in.."* ?
   Albert Campion

4.) For what sleuthing purpose does Lord Peter Wimsey affect a monocle?
   It's a magnifying lens

5.) Who said *"..I landed in Labrador from a friend's yacht once, and the man in the village store said: You wear your moustache shorter now, Sgt.."* ?
   Alan Grant

6.) Whose first case, in 1921, was called *"The Attenbury Emeralds"* ?
   Peter Wimsey

7.) Hercule Poirot was originally a policeman in Belgium. What rank had he achieved when he retired?
   Chief of Police

8.) Which sleuth says the purpose behind undertaking an investigation is *"..to find the truth and serve justice, not prove innocence or guilt.."* ?
Maud Silver
9.) Who saved his brother's life by proving a murder accusation false?
Peter Wimsey
10.) Who often refers to *"The Case of the Soap Manufacturer of Lieges"*, a man who poisoned his wife in order to marry his blonde secretary?
Hercule Poirot
11.) Which sleuth's first case was *"The Urtingham Pearls"* ?
Maud Silver
12.) Which sleuth claims to have *"..special gifts of observation.."*, of *"..knowing human nature.."*, of being *"..able to draw parallels from village life.."* ?
Jane Marple
13.) Which sleuth commits a murder?
Hercule Poirot
14.) Which sleuth determines criminals *"..by the look of their face.."* and has never lost a case?
Alan Grant
15.) Which sleuth met his future wife at her murder trial?
Peter Wimsey
16.) Which sleuth believes that women generally *"..do not appreciate the abstract passion for justice.."* ?
Maud Silver

17.) Hercule Poirot once retired and planned to grow what in his garden?
Perfect vegetable marrows

18.) Which sleuth frequently refers to the intriguingly titled *"Case of the Poisoned Caterpillars"* ?
Maud Silver

19.) Roderick Alleyn became *"..the youngest Chief Inspector in Scotland Yard history.."* at what age?
43

20.) Which sleuth's first case was *"The Crime at Black Dudley"* ?
Albert Campion

21.) Who taught Miss Maud Silver how to shoot a pistol?
Agnes Fane's father

22.) Which sleuth turned down the Governorship of an island?
Albert Campion

23.) Tommy and Tuppence Beresford run Blunt's Brilliant Detectives on behalf of the owner who is a friend of whom?
Mr Carter

24.) Miss Jane Marple is able to solve the mystery of *"The Four Suspects"* because her German governess taught her what Victorian skill?
The Language of Flowers

25.) Which sleuth served in the Diplomatic Corps from 1919-1920 and speaks conversational French and Italian?
Roderick Alleyn

ANSWERS
Chapter 5 - Cars

1.) What kind of car does Lugg acquire in later life?
   a Morris Minor
2.) In what Ngaio Marsh novel would you find a local taxi called *"The Bloodbath"* ?
   Hand in Glove
3.) Who owns a car they find very difficult to get out of?
   Ariadne Oliver
4.) Who are the three sleuths who do not drive?
   Hercule Poirot, Maud Silver, and Jane Marple
5.) What kind of car does Hercule Poirot own?
   Messarro-Gratz
6.) At this sleuth's first appearance he can't afford to run a car but later acquires a Lagonda then a Bentley. Who is he?
   Albert Campion
7.) By what name does Lord Peter Wimsey call his Daimlers?
   Mrs Merdle
8.) Of which sleuth's car is it said *"..there's one gear..any other handle you pull you get your money back.."* ?
   Albert Campion
9.) What does Valentine Ferris (Albert Campion's sister) call her car?
   The Running Footman
10.) What is the name of the taxi-driver from Miss Jane Marple's village?

Young Inch

ANSWERS
Chapter 6 – Clubs

1.) What are the names of Albert Campion's three clubs?
   Junior Grays, Boiled Owl, Puffins
2.) What are the names of Lord Peter Wimsey's three clubs?
   Egotists, Marlborough, Bellona
3.) Whose club is *"The United Arts"* ?
   Troy

ANSWERS
Chapter 7 - Education

1.) Which sleuth's house at Oxford was *"Davidsons"* ?
   Roderick Alleyn
2.) As a child which sleuth attended *"Botolph's Abbey"* ?
   Albert Campion
3.) Which sleuth's cousin is married to his school roommate and best friend?
   Alan Grant
4.) Which sleuth was taught by a German governess?
   Jane Marple
5.) Which sleuth was a governess for twenty years?
   Maud Silver
6.) In University which sleuth was nicknamed *"The Great Flim"* ?
   Peter Wimsey
7.) Which sleuth went to *"St Agatha's, Oxford"* and *"St Ignatius College, Cambridge"* ?
   Albert Campion
8.) Whose teacher was *"Old Miss Payne"* ?
   Ernest Lamb
9.) Who *"..was taught knitting in the Continental manner by Fraulein Stein.."* ?
   Maud Silver
10.) Which sleuth was sent to *"..a pensionnat in Florence.."* ?
   Jane Marple
11.) Which sleuth took a First reading History at Balliol?

Peter Wimsey
12.) Which sleuth studied at the Bar until a family dispute ended the funding of his legal career?
Frank Abbott
13.) Which sleuth claims the school motto of *"Floreat Fauna"* stood for *"grow, you little beasts"* ?
Albert Campion
14.) Which sleuth enjoyed illicit after-hours feasts with schoolfriend Cecelia Voycey?
Maud Silver

ANSWERS
Chapter 8 - Family

1.) What is Albert's true first name?
Rudolph
2.) Which of Maud Silver's nieces, Ethel and Gladys, is the elder?
Gladys
3.) To which career does Ricky Alleyn aspire?
Writer
4.) Whose father died in the Crimean War?
Amanda Fitton
5.) Who is Lord Peter Wimsey's ward?
Hilary Thorpe
6.) Whose daughter is called Hattie but "..his wife preferred Atalanta.." ?
Charlie Luke
7.) Jane's niece-in-law, Joan West, is aunt to whom?
Louise Oxley
8.) Albert's sister Valentine was disinherited for her marriage to Sidney Ferris. Who is her second husband?
Alan Dell
9.) What was the married name of Lugg's sister?
Beatt Bowels
10.) What are the names of the three children of Tommy and Tuppence Beresford?
Derek, Deborah, and Betty
11.) What was the maiden name of Roderick Alleyn's mother?
Blandish

12.) What is the name of Albert and Amanda Campion's son?
Rupert
13.) What is the name of Laura Rankin's, (cousin of Alan Grant), son?
Patrick
14.) What are the names of Miss Maud Silver's parents?
Maria and Alfred
15.) Who claims to be: *"..a renegade Scot. My grandfather belonged to Strathspey.."* ?
Alan Grant
16.) Who is the niece of Roderick Alleyn involved in a murder during her Coming-Out season?
Sarah Alleyn
17.) In which book do we actually meet Sir George Alleyn?
"**Black As He's Painted"**

ANSWERS
Chapter 9 – Friends & Cohorts

1.) In the Short Story *"The Blue Geranium"* Miss Jane Marple and Dolly Bantry are mere acquaintances, but by the time of which novel they are great friends?
   "The Body in the Library"
2.) Miss Maud Silver's *"dearest friend"* was Mary Meredith. What is the name of Mary's daughter?
   Ruth Ball
3.) What is the name of Albert Campion's American friend who teaches History?
   Professor Carey
4.) What are the names of the erudite vicar and his *"terrifying wife"* who are good friends of Miss Jane Marple?
   Maud and Caleb Dane Calthorpe
5.) Which friend of Albert Campion's inherited a family business that includes the forging of antique jewelry?
   Israel Mechizadek
6.) Rietta Cray and Randal March, (friends of Miss Maud Silver), eventually marry and raise a family. What are the names of their children?
   George and Meg
7.) Who is Albert Campion's disreputable dancing-master friend *"..thin, elderly and affected.."* with a Studio in Cavendish Square?
   Beaut Siegfried
8.) What newspaper does Lord Peter Wimsey's friend Salcombe Hardy work for?

The Daily Yell
9.) What is Colonel Race's, (friend to Hercule Poirot), Christian name?
John
10.) What are the names of Marta Hallard's parents?
Anne and Gervase Wing-Strutt
11.) Who is Troy's best friend?
Katti Bostock
12.) What is the name of Roderick Alleyn's *"friendly newshound"* ?
Nigel Bathgate
13.) What is the name of the Police-Surgeon Roderick Alleyn always requests?
Dr. Curtis, later Sir James Curtis

ANSWERS
Chapter 10 – Habits

1.) Who has "..*a child's waterpistol fashioned to look like a revolver..*" ?
   Albert Campion
2.) Who has the "..*habit of moistening his forefinger when turning a page..*" ?
   Inspector Fox
3.) Which two sleuths don't smoke?
   Jane Marple and Maud Silver
4.) Who has "..*spiky, spidery handwriting heavily-underlined.. like a spider in an ink bottle..*" ?
   Jane Marple
5.) Who has distinctive handwriting "..*square with heavy downstrokes and sharp Greek Es..*"
   Albert Campion
6.) Who takes sugar, never saccharine, in coffee but only milk in tea?
   Maud Silver
7.) Who drinks hot chocolate instead of tea?
   Hercule Poirot
8.) Which sleuth claims "..*to have no truck with doctors and their medicines.. grandmother's tansy tea is equal to any amount of drugs..*" ?
   Jane Marple
9.) Who has a penchant for munching on apples?
   Ariadne Oliver
10.) Who buys pyjamas from Dodds "..*altered to have a piece of flannel sewn across the shoulderblades..*" ?

Albert Campion
11.) Who smokes tiny Russian cigarettes?
Hercule Poirot
12.) Who can't stand hearing foreign languages spoken?
Ernest Lamb
13.) Who collects First Editions?
Peter Wimsey
14.) Whose favourite colour is bright blue, and second favourite is pink?
Maud Silver
15.) Who thinks a square egg would be ideal?
Hercule Poirto
16.) Who only reads the Obituaries section of The Times?
Lugg
17.) Which sleuth "..*sends the plate and the King Charles tankard to the bank and puts the maid on board-wages..*" while away?
Jane Marple
18.) Who wears only black patent-leather shoes - even in the country?
Hercule Poirot
19.) Whose tailor is Jamieson & Fellowes?
Albert Campion
20.) Which sleuth is a lifelong avid gardener?
Jane Marple
21.) What is Miss Maud Silver's nightly bedtime reading?
The Bible

ANSWERS
Chapter 11 – Matchmaking

Agatha Troy	Roderick Alleyn
Amanda Fitton	Albert Campion
Angela North	Nigel Bathgate
Bridget Paget	Marlowe Lobbett
Cicely Abbott	Grant Hathaway
Dulcibella Duveen	Arthur Hastings
Harriet Vane	Peter Wimsey
Henrietta Cray	Randall March
Isobel Lobbett	Giles Paget
Janet Pursuivant	Gilbert Whippet
Joan/Joyce Lempriere	Raymond West
Margaret Langton	Charles Moray
Mary Fitton	Augustus Randall
Mary Wimsey	Charles Parker
Nicola Maitland-Mayne	Andrew Bantling
Prudence Cowley	Thomas Beresford
Rachel Levy	Frederick Arbuthnot
Valentine Ferris	Alan Dell
Victoria Prunella Scroop-Dory	Charles Luke

ANSWERS
Chapter 12 – Nicknames & Aliases

1.) P.E. Garbel, a relation of Agatha Troy's, calls Troy and Rory... what?
   Aggie and Roddy
2.) Who is known as *"Pickled Gherkin"*?
   Gerry Wimsey
3.) What friend of Roderick Alleyn's is nicknamed *"Bunchy"* ?
   Sir Robert Gospell
4.) Who calls Albert Campion *"..Orph.. short for Orpheus as in Orpheus and his Lute.."* ?
   Amanda Fitton
5.) Who is called *"Cid"* by his son?
   Roderick Alleyn
6.) Captain Arthur Hastings calls his wife *"Cinderella"*, what is her real name?
   Dulcibella Duveen
7.) Who is called *"Uncle Beastly"* ?
   Lugg
8.) Who is Roderick Alleyn's schoolmate nicknamed *"The Boomer"* ?
   Bartholomew Opala
9.) Who named his beard *"..impudence, persuasion out of cheek.."* ?
   Albert Campion
10.) Who is *"Miss Robinson"* ?
   Tuppence Beresford
11.) Who is the English crook called *"The Destroyer"* detected by Hercule Poirot?
   Claud Darrel
12.) Who calls Miss Jane Marple *"Nemesis"* ?
   Mr Rafiel

13.) What is Albert Campion's Christian name?
Rudolph
14.) Who is C.J. Broderick?
Roderick Alleyn
15.) What do Albert Campion and friends call the elderly Lady Larradine?
"Old Lady 'ell"
16.) Whose surname is translated as *"Vainse"*
Peter Wimsey
17.) Mrs Sarah, matriarch of the Gypsies, calls Albert Campion… what?
Orlando
18.) Who is Death Bredon?
Peter Wimsey
19.) Who do the newspapers call *"The Handsome Sleuth"* ?
Roderick Alleyn
20.) Who is *"Maggers"* ?
Lugg
21.) Who is *"Birdie"* ?
Inspector Fox
22.) Who is *"Polly"* ?
Mary Wimsey
23.) Who is *"Lalla"* ?
Laura Rankin
24.) Who is *"Br'er Fox"* ?
Inspector Fox
25.) What shortening of his name does Albert Campion detest?
Bert
26.) Fill in the blanks on these AKAs of Albert Campion:
Christopher **Twelvetrees**
Mr **Mornington** Dodd

The Hon. **Tootles** Ash
Albert **Memorial**
Evan Booth

27.) What is the real name of Tuppence Beresford?
Prudence

28.) Who is Septimus Falls?
Roderick Alleyn

29.) Who is Patricia Blenkensop?
Tuppence Beresford

ANSWERS
Chapter 13 – Old Tragedies

1.) Which book refers to the Opera "Lucia di Lammermoor" ?
   "The Ivory Dagger"
2.) Which book refers to the Play *"The Duchess of Malfi"* ?
   "Sleeping Murder"
3.) Which book tells of Sandra Compline who had a wax face-lift by Franz Hartz to regain her straying husband but the surgery didn't take and the result was disastrous?
   "Death and the Dancing Footman"
4.) Which book tells of Hal Huntingforest marrying Mary Fitton the day before he left for the Crimean War where he was killed but Mary's mother-in-law, Josephine, forces the young Vicar to destroy the marriage record?
   "Danger Point"
5.) Which book tells the story that during the war Ludovic Danberry-Phinn, private secretary to Sir Harold Lackland, is wrongly accused of treason and commits suicide?
   "Scales of Justice"
6.) Which books tells of James Barton, badly wounded in the Far East, returning home from war to find his wife living with another man and when he killed them both being sent to the Asylum for the Criminally Insane at Broadmoor?
   "Poison in the Pen"

7.) Which book tells the tale of a vendetta between the Pepitone and Rossi families where only women are killed, beginning with *"..the murder of a Pepitone girl by her Rossi bridegroom.."* ?
    "Photo Finish"

ANSWERS
Chapter 14 – Personal Staff

1.) What is the name of Roderick Alleyn's manservant?
   Vassily
2.) Who was his previous employer?
   Sir Hubert Handesley
3.) What is the name of the boy-turned-manservant of Tommy and Tuppence Beresford?
   Albert
4.) What was his previous employment?
   Lift-operator in a block of flats
5.) What is the full name of Albert Campion's manservant?
   Magersfontein Lugg
6.) What was his previous employment?
   Burglar
7.) What is the full name of Lord Peter Wimsey's manservant?
   Mervyn Bunter
8.) Who was his previous employer?
   Sir John Sanderton
9.) Name Alan Grant's daily?
   Mrs Tinker
10.) What was her previous employment?
   Theatre Dresser
11.) Who was the *"Domestic Engineer"* Raymond West hired after Miss Jane Marple's bout with pneumonia?
   Lucy Eylesbarrow
12.) What is the surname of Miss Jane Marple's *"Faithful Florence"* ?

Knight

13.) What are the two names (due to an editing error) by which Miss Maud Silver's housekeeper is called?
Emma and Hannah Meadows

14.) What is the name of Albert Campion's family chauffeur?
Wootten

15.) Who is Mr Satterthwaite's chauffeur?
Masters

16.) What does Hercule Poirot call his manservant?
Georges

17.) Tommy and Tuppence Beresford's manservant eventually grows up, marries Amy and they open a pub. What are the names of their three children?
Charlie, Jean, and Elizabeth

18.) What was Lugg's post during WWII?
Heavy Rescue Civil Defence, ARP

19.) Cherry and Jim Baker originally came from Huddersfield. Before they moved in with Miss Jane Marple they lived at what address in *"The Development"* ?
16 Aubrey Close

20.) Who is Bunter's *"..only relative.."* ?
His mother

21.) Except in a different novel we learn that Bunter is one of.. how many?
Seven

22.) How old was Albert Campion when he acquired Lugg?
Eighteen

23.) Hercule Poirot's secretary, Miss Lemon, dreams of developing the perfect.. what?
    Filing System
24.) What is the name of Alan Grant's landlady?
    Mrs Fields

ANSWERS
Chapter 15 – Personal Trivia

1.) Who "..looks like a cross between a monk and a grandee - more grandee in evening clothes.." ?
   Roderick Alleyn
2.) Who has a penchant for buying hats?
   Tuppence Beresford
3.) Who was born on May 20th, 1900?
   Albert Campion
4.) who has "..according to co-workers, only two weaknesses 'coffee and coffee'.." ?
   Alan Grant
5.) Who maintains "..a bank balance of 444 pounds, 4 shillings and 4 pence.." ?
   Hercule Poirot
6.) Who "..runs in an odd, hen-like manner.." ?
   Maud Silver
7.) Whose phone number is 395?
   Jane Marple
8.) Who was born in 1896?
   Roderick Alleyn
9.) Who has twins born in 1929?
   Tuppence and Tommy Beresford
10.) Whose birthday is August 4th?
   Alan Grant
11.) Who is constantly redesigning her hair into elaborate styles?
   Ariadne Oliver
12.) Who based his new career on information learned during 35 years as a civil servant?
   Parker Pyne

13.) Who *"..looks like an athletic don with a hint of the Army somewhere.."*
Roderick Alleyn
14.) Alan Grant claims his palate is his *"..most precious possession.."* and, as a result, never eats.. what?
Pickles
15.) Who was called *"..a cross between a bear and a baby and exhibited the most pleasing traits of both creatures.."* ?
Inspector Fox
16.) Who always travels with a pair of curling tongs?
Hercule Poirot
17.) Who has *"..brown, slightly protuberant eyes like large peppermint bulleyes.."* ?
Chief-Inspector Ernest Lamb
18.) Hercule Poirot and Mr Satterthwaite share what common malady?
Seasickness
19.) Who wears pince-nez for *"..occasional use for very fine print.."* ?
Maud Silver
20.) Who is Albert Campion's Doctor?
Old Todd of Wimpole Street
21.) Who is Lord Peter Wimsey's Doctor?
Sir Julian Freke
22.) Which sleuth suffers from claustrophobia?
Alan Grant

ANSWERS
Chapter 16 – Policemen

1.) Which policeman has "..*a face carved out of wood..*"?
   Superintendent Battle
2.) What is Superintendent Yeo's Christian name?
   Freddie
3.) Who is Superintendent Battle's policeman nephew?
   James (Jim) Leach
4.) Who is Sir Henry Clithering's policeman godson?
   Detective-Inspector Dermot Craddock
5.) What is Chief-Superintendent Oates Christian name?
   Stanislau
6.) Who is Chief-Superintendent Oates secretary?
   Sergeant Tovey
7.) Which policeman spends years learning French from home study courses?
   Inspector Fox
8.) This policeman's youngest (of five) children was accused of theft by Miss Amphrey, headmistress of Meadway.
   Superintendent Battle
9.) Identify Chief-Inspector Ernest Lamb's three daughters.
   Violet, Myrtle, and Lily
10.) Which policeman has "..*gray cold eyes as bleak as the North Sea..*"?

Chief-Superintendent Oates
11.) Which policeman's hangout is "..the Coach and Horses pub at the wrong end of Early Street.." ?
Superintendent Yeo
12.) What is the name of Chief-Superintendent Oates wife?
Marion, sometimes Mary
13.) Whose pet phrase is "..we'll have to get you into the force.." ?
Inspector Fox
14.) Who is Alan Grant's boss?
Bryce, sometimes Barker
15.) Alan Grant's sergeant, Williams, is married to Nora. Name their two children.
Angela and Leonard
16.) Due to his contempt for "..fancy-dress coppers.." which policeman's only disguise is "..an ancient Donegal tweed ulster and an out-of-date felt hat.." which makes him look like "..a North of Ireland corn chandler on holiday.." ?
Inspector Fox
17.) In what book does Albert Campion meet Inspector Charlie Luke?
"More Work for the Undertaker"
18.) At the age of 43 he is "..the youngest chief-inspector at the Central Branch of New Scotland Yard.."
Roderick Alleyn
19.) What is the full name of Inspector Fox?
Edward (Teddy) Walter Fox

ANSWERS
Chapter 17 – Publications

1.) *"Notes for Collectors of Incunabula"*.
   Peter Wimsey
2.) *"The Body in the Library"* (NOT the Agatha Christie version).
   Ariadne Oliver
3.) *"Principles and Practise of Criminal Investigation"*.
   Roderick Alleyn
4.) *"Death in the Pot"*.
   Harriet Vane
5.) *"The Affair of the Second Goldfish"*.
   Ariadne Oliver
6.) Who wanted to write *"The Mystery of the Second Cucumber"* ?
   Antony Eastwood
7.) *"The History of Bells at Fenchurch St. Paul"*.
   Reverend Christopher Woollcott
8.) *"The Duchess of Malfi"*.
   John Webster
9.) *"The Murderer's Compendium"*.
   Peter Wimsey
10.) *"Crabbed Age and Youth"*.
   Jeremy Skelton
11.) *"Angelo in August"*.
   Sebastian Mailer
12.) *"Simon in Latium"*.
   Barnaby Grant
13.) *"The Death in the Drainpipe"*.
   Ariadne Oliver
14.) *"Memoirs of an Old Buffer"*.

William Farraday
15.) Who are Roderick Alleyn's publishers?
Brierley and Bentwood
16.) Whose fictional sleuth is called *"Sven Hjerson"* ?
Ariadne Oliver
17.) Whose fictional sleuth is called *"Robert Templeton"* ?
Harriet Vane
18.) What's the name of the local newspaper at Gyrth and Pontisbright?
East Suffolk Courier and Hadleigh Argus
19.) What's the name of the local newspaper at St Mary Mead?
Daily Newsgiver
20.) What's the name of the local newspaper at Chipping Cleghorn?
The North Benham News and Chipping Cleghorn Gazette
21.) The play *"Little Mary"* made Miss Jane Marple and Colonel Easterly blush. Who wrote it?
Sir James M. Barrie
22.) Who is the author behind pen name Aubrey Mandrake?
Stanley Footling
23.) Which novelist and noted poet writes without capital letters?
Raymond West
24.) What old book does Lord Peter Wimsey's nephew, Jerry, buy which contains a map of buried treasure?

Munster's Cosmographia Universalis
25.) Who claims to have written *"Character from Characters, or How to Tell Your Lover by his Note"* ?
Albert Campion
26.) Who writes a newspaper column called *"..The Helping Hand.. ask G.P.F. (Guide, Philosopher, Friend) about it.."* ?
Lord Pastern and Bagott
27.) Who promises Albert Campion *"..an illuminated address of 5,000 words, written in my own hand, and coloured.."* if Albert catches a society blackmailer?
Chief-Superintendent Oates
28.) Who is writing the novel *"Elephants do Forget"* ?
Edmund Swettenham
29.) Harriet Vane was able to afford her wedding gift to Lord Peter Wimsey by writing a 3,500 word short story for what publication?
Thrill Magazine
30.) Who wrote *"Under the Fig Tree"* and is currently writing *"Snow on the Desert's Face"* ?
Salome Otterbourne
31.) Who said, of detective novelists, *"..he heads one chapter 'Routine', dismisses six weeks of drudgery in as many phrases, cuts the cackle and gets to the 'osses. I wish to the Lord we could follow his lead.."* ?
Roderick Alleyn
32.) Who wrote *"The Scaly Breed"* ?
Colonel Maurice Cartarette

33.) Which Lethal Lady wrote *"Unpopular Opinions"* ?
   Dorothy L. Sayers
34.) Which Lethal Lady's autobiography is called *"Come, Tell Me How You Live"* ?
   Agatha Christie
35.) Which Lethal Lady's autobiography is called *"Black Beech and Honeydew"* ?
   Ngaio Marsh

ANSWERS
Chapter 18 – Quotes

1.) "..inexperienced young women are sadly liable to be carried away by specious arguments on the subject of free union and companionate marriage. They fail to realize until too late that though civilized marriage laws may sometimes prove irksome, they nevertheless exist for the protection of women and family.."
Maud Silver

2.) "..it casts a spurious but acceptable glamour over the more squalid aspects of my profession.."
Roderick Alleyn

3.) "..when I know what the murderer is like, I shall be able to find out who he is.."
Hercule Poirot

4.) "..if anyone over the age of sixty-five finds fault with you never argue. Never try to say you're right. Apologize at once and say it was all your fault and you're very sorry and you'll never do it again.."
Tuppence Beresford

5.) "..I always believe the worst. What is so sad is that one is usually justified in doing so.."
Jane Marple

6.) "..would it invite confidence more, d'you suppose, if I dyed my hair black an' grew a Newgate fringe? It's very trying', you can't think, always to look as if one's name was Algy.."

Peter Wimsey
7.) *"..as far as.. was concerned the human race was glass-fronted, and, furthermore that.. saw right past the shop-window into the back premises.."*
Maud Silver
8.) *"..he was , I might almost say, exceptionally ordinary-looking.. sleek, pale hair, and one of those rather stupid faces with a long nose and monocle.."*
Peter Wimsey
9.) When asked if he'd heard of *"The Rape of Lucrece"* replied: *"I can't say I have unless it's on the police list which it sounds as if it might be. Or would it be Shakespeare?"*
Inspector Fox
10.) *"..last time I saw him we walked down Regent Street together, and from the corner of Conduit Street to the Circus we met five people he knew, including a Viscountess and two Bishops. Each of them stopped and greeted him as an old pal and every single one of them called him by a different name.."*
Albert Campion
11.) *"..is just the finest detective God ever made. Natural genius cultivated in a suitable soil.."*
Jane Marple
12.) *"..a dark handsome deeply bronzed man of fifty, he was usually to be found in some outpost of the Empire - especially if there were trouble brewing.."*
Colonel Race

13.) *"..you don't even have to say: 'Hop it!' You just look at them, and they begin to recollect appointments.."*
    Alan Grant

ANSWERS
Chapter 19 – Religion

1.) Which sleuth "*..not for the first time felt his own lack of acceptance to be tinged with a faint regret..*" ?
   Roderick Alleyn
2.) Which sleuth is one of a Country Vicar's five daughters?
   Tuppence Beresford
3.) Whose mother belongs to the Church Militant?
   Albert Campion
4.) Who considers fishing "*..a cross between a sport and a religion..*" ?
   Alan Grant
5.) Who lives next door to a Vicarage?
   Jane Marple
6.) Whose Victoria tea-set is missing one cup "*..broken by Great-Aunt Louisa's Vicar when he slammed it into its saucer to emphasize his point that Eve's sin forced subjugation on all women..*" ?
   Maud Silver
7.) Whose uncle was the Bishop of Ely?
   Jane Marple
8.) Whose uncle was Canon of St. Peter the Gate?
   Albert Campion
9.) Whose godfather was the Bishop of Devizes?
   Albert Campion
10.) Whose uncle was the Canon of Chichester Cathedral?

Jane Marple
11.) Who is a Catholic who *"..strongly believes in the force of superstition.."* ?
Hercule Poirot
12.) The text *"Ask And Ye Shall Receive"* was pinned over whose childhood bed?
Jane Marple
13.) A modern painting of a Madonna and Child seemed to which sleuth's *"..simple, evangelical mind.. an abominable blasphemy.."* ?
Charles Parker
14.) Who reads a portion of Scripture every night?
Maud Silver
15.) What is the name of the Church at Duke's Denver?
St John act-Portam-Latinam

ANSWERS
Chapter 20 – Romance

1.) Who married someone else because she thought Albert Campion was "..*comic about women..*"?
   Biddy Paget
2.) Which confirmed bachelor almost proposed when in Kew Gardens "..*to see the bluebells..*"
   Mr Satterthwaite
3.) Whose mother hoped her son would marry Evelyn Curtis, daughter of her greatest friend?
   Roderick Alleyn
4.) Who keeps photo mementos of the couples brought together as a result of successful sleuthing?
   Maud Silver
5.) What was Troy painting when she met Roderick?
   The Wharf at Suva
6.) Albert Campion keeps "..*a small, yellow-flowered button from her dress..*" .. whose?
   Linda Sutane
7.) What was the name of Lord Peter Wimsey's first fiancee?
   Barbara
8.) Who calls Albert Campion *"The Universal Aunt"*?
   Amanda Fitton
9.) Alan Grant met which woman when her pearls were stolen?
   Marta Hallard
10.) Who was Harriet Vane's live-in lover?
   Philip Boyes

11.) Whose fiance was murdered and her brother charged with the crime?
Mary Wimsey
12.) Whose Aunt Primrose "..had been in and out of 11 Nursing Homes.." before falling in love with the much-younger Mervyn and planned to set up house with him in Aberdeen until he was arrested?
Tuppence Beresford
13.) Who was the Best Man at Harriet and Peter's wedding?
Saint-George, Gerry Wimsey, Jr.
14.) Whose daughter was Lugg once engaged to?
Wardie Sampson, a forger
15.) With what words does Troy accept Roderick Alleyn's proposal?
"I won't be parked"
16.) What words did Peter Wimsey say when he proposed, and was accepted, by Harriet Vane?
"Placetne, Magistra?"

ANSWERS
Chapter 21 – Scotland Yard

1.) Who is "..*Father Superior of the second most tough police division in Metro London and proud of it..*" ?
Charlie Luke
2.) Who is godfather to Chief-Superintendent Oates son?
Albert Campion
3.) Who has Room 49 at the Yard?
Superintendent Yeo
4.) When asked if he's "..*the star turn at Scotland Yard..*" who replies: "..*oh no.. I come in bundles..*" ?
Alan Grant
5.) When Roderick Alleyn calls for *"Flash and Dabs"* (Photographer and Fingerprinter), who does he get?
Thompson and Bailey
6.) What is the phone number of New Scotland Yard?
Whitehall 1212 or WHI ABAB

ANSWERS
Chapter 22 – Sherlock Holmes

1.) Who said *"..I think part of the charm of those excellent tales lies in Watson's casual but enthralling references to cases we never hear of again.."* ?
Roderick Alleyn
2.) Who does the Daily Mirror call *"The Sherlock Holmes of the West End"* ?
Peter Wimsey
3.) Who said *"..I'm an old-fashioned woman and I call it mother-wit, and it's so rare for a man to have it that if he does you write a book about him and call him Sherlock Holmes.."* ?
Honoria, Dowager Duchess of Denver *(Peter Wimsey's mother)*
4.) Sergeant Williams, at the age of eleven, hid *"..in a hayloft in Worchestershire trying to read _____ without being discovered by Authority, who had banned it.."* What Sherlock Holmes story was he reading?
"The Speckled Band"

ANSWERS
Chapter 23 – Sports & Games

1.) Cricket
   "Murder Must Advertise"
2.) Fishing (two books)
   "Scales of Justice"
   "The Singing Sands"
3.) Gymnastics
   "Miss Pym Disposes"
4.) Tennis
   "Cat Among The Pigeons"
5.) Bridge
   "Cards on the Table"
6.) Mah Jongg
   "The Murder of Roger Ackroyd"
7.) Golf
   "Murder on the Links"
8.) The Murder Game (three books)
   "The Crime at Black Dudley"
   "Dead Man's Folly"
   "A Man Lay Dead"
9.) A Darts game of Round-the-Clock
   "Death at the Bar"

ANSWERS
Chapter 24 – St Mary Mead

1.) What is the County?
   Much Benham
2.) What is the Shire?
   Downshire
3.) Where is the closest Train Station?
   Milchester
4.) What are the names of the four Taxi Companies?
   Young Inch
   Pip's Cars
   James Taxis
   Arthur's Car Hire
5.) What are the names of the two Doctors?
   Dr Haydock
   Dr Sanford
6.) What is the name of the local Manor?
   Gossington Hall
7.) What is the name of the local Orphanage?
   St Faith's
8.) What is the name of the local Inn?
   The Blue Boar
9.) Who is the Coroner?
   Dr Roberts
10.) What is the name of the local Bank?
   Middleton's
11.) Who is the Oldest Inhabitant?
   Mr Sampson
12.) Who is the Gardener?
   Old Laycock
13.) Who is the Grocer?
   Barnes

14.) What is the name of the new suburb?
The Development
15.) What is the name of the Constable?
Hurst
16.) What are the names of the two Inspectors?
Inspector Frank Cornish
Inspector Slack
17.) Who is the Chief Constable?
Colonel Melchett
18.) What is the name of the Curate?
Mr Hawes

ANSWERS
Chapter 25 – Trivial Trivia

1.) What direction is *"widdershins"* ?
   Counter-clockwise
2.) *"Dactylography"* is the study of what?
   Fingerprinting
3.) Who wrote *"The Bride of Lammermoor"* ?
   Sir Walter Scott
4.) Which French gentleman invented the *"Portrait Parle"* and the *"Fingerprint Theory"* ?
   Bertillon
5.) Which peer created the Police College?
   Lord Trenchard
6.) What is the name of the Police College?
   Hendon
7.) In what textbook would you find:
   What was the crime? Who did it?
   When was it done? and Where?
   How done? and with what motive?
   Who on the deed did share?
   Gross's Criminal Psychology
8.) Every English county has a Criminal Investigation Division (C.I.D). If they call in Scotland Yard who pays the investigation cost?
   If the Yard is called within 3 days the CID pays, otherwise it's the County Council.
9.) What are *"Hudson's Processes"* ?
   Lifting fingerprints from cloth or wool with silver nitrate.
10.) In Miss Jane Marple's time what did the word banting mean?

Dieting

11.) In what book would one find the litany:
   *From Envy, Hatred, Malice
   and all Uncharitableness
   Good Lord deliver us*

The Church of England's "Book of Common Prayer"

12.) What was the name of the Times critic and crossword puzzler constructor during the war years? and who was his successor?

   Torquemada, then Ximenes

13.) In the Vehicle Registry the name listed on the documents is called what?

   The Keeper

14.) In Alan Grant's time it was illegal for stores to sell this after 9:00 pm.

   Tobacco/Cigarettes

15.) Crime Writers formed *"The Detective Club"* in 1932. Which of the Lethal Ladies was its second president, holding the office for nine years?

   Dorothy L. Sayers

16.) Who and what was the club mascot?

   Eric the Skull

17.) Translate the following Latin:
   Quomodo Quando Quibis Auxillis

   How, When, With What

18.) Debretts, Burkes and Landed Gentry are the Who's Who of the British Aristocracy. What is the Continental version called?

   Almanac de Gotha

19.) What is a *"campion"* ?

   a **flower**

20.) What is the English word for the French word *"chantage"* ?
    blackmail
21.) English Policeman cannot drink or.. what? while on duty?
    Smoke
22.) The *"Ingolldsby Legends"* tell the tale of the *"Hand of Glory"* (from the *"Compendium Maleficonum"*). What is it?
    Hand cut from the corpse of a felon or a murdered man.
23.) What do the initials V.A.D represent?
    Voluntary Aid Department
24.) Name the Artist who painted the covers of Agatha Christie's books.
    Tom Adams
25.) Legal Aid available to the British needy is called what?
    Poor Persons Defence Act
26.) This Latin phrase *"Quis, Quid, Ubi, Quius Auxiliis, Cur, Quomondo, Quando"* is known as the what?
    The Jurists Maxim
27.) To what are the stories referring when they use the word receipt?
    a recipe
28.) What are the Seven Deadly Sins?
    Avarice
    Envy
    Gluttony
    Lust
    Pride
    Sloth
    Wrath

29.) What are the Seven Virtues?
- **Charity**
- **Faith**
- **Fortitude**
- **Hope**
- **Justice**
- **Prudence**
- **Temperance**

ANSWERS
Chapter 26 – Unusual Weapons

1.) Blunt Instrument: a jeroboam of champagne.
   "Vintage Murder"
2.) Deadly spray in a nasal inhaler.
   "The Mirror Crack'd"
3.) A Russian dagger used during a game of Murder.
   "A Man Lay Dead"
4.) A ceremonial African spear.
   "Black as he's Painted"
5.) A gun placed inside a piano and hooked to the soft pedal.
   "Overture to Death"
6.) A silver-plated skewer through the eye.
   "A Surfeit of Lampreys"
7.) A Chinese dagger once owned by Marco Polo.
   "The Ivory Dagger"
8.) Cyanide in the stem of a pipe.
   "Police at the Funeral"
9.) Weed-killer in a perfume atomizer.
   "False Scent"

ANSWERS
Chapter 27 – Wartime

1.) Who attained the rank of Major in WWI?
   Peter Wimsey
2.) During WWI Albert Campion was in the Afghanistan Campaign. How long did he serve?
   The last 6 months of the war.
3.) Why did Frank Abbott have four applications to the RAF rejected?
   He was needed as a policeman.
4.) During WWII a bomb exploded on Miss Maud Silver's street. What damage was done to her apartment?
   It broke the windows and tore the curtains.
5.) After being wounded on the Belgian Front in WWI who was invalided out to serve as a Recruiting Officer?
   Captain Hastings
6.) From which branch of the forces was Chief Inspector Lamb refused in WWI?
   Army
7.) Who was Tommy Beresford's superior, nicknamed *"Old Josh"* ?
   Maj-Gen Sir Josiah Penn
8.) Who suffered a breakdown lasting two years after being buried in *"..a shell-hole at Caudry.."* ?
   Peter Wimsey
9.) Where was Albert Campion during WWII?
   Beirut

10.) Who was "..trapped in the Antipodes.. tracking Fifth Columnists?
Roderick Alleyn
11.) What was Tommy Beresford's rank in WWI?
Lieutenant
12.) What war work did Troy perform for the Army?
Camouflage and pictorial surveys
13.) What did Amanda Campion refer to as her *"war work"*?
Her son Rupert
14.) What was the name of the General Tuppence Beresford drove during WWI?
Francis Haviland
15.) What was the name of the Boarding-House where Tuppence Beresford posed as a twice-married woman with three sons?
Sans Souci
16.) Who is the subject of this quote: *"..He belonged to a post-war generation, that particular generation which was too young for one war and most prematurely too old for the next.. His was the age which had never known illusion, the grimly humourous generation which from childhood had both expected and experienced the seamier side.."* ?
Albert Campion
17.) Who spent *"..four years on the Western Front.."* ?
Alan Grant
18.) Who was Troy painting when Roderick Alleyn returned home?
Sir Henry Ancred as MacBeth

ANSWERS
Chapter 28 – Wills & Epitaphs

1.) Roderick Alleyn's French Teacher, Miss Emily Pride, inherited.. what? from her sister Fanny Bottom?
   Portcarrow Island
2.) Who was the sole beneficiary of a fortune because *"..she is too young to be mercenary.."* ?
   Cicely Hathaway
3.) Who left Miss Jane Marple a legacy of 20,000 pounds sterling if she would fulfill a commission?
   Mr Rafiel
4.) From whom did Miss Maud Silver inherit her carved bog-oak rose brooch?
   Aunt Editha Blake
5.) The Bishop of Devizes received a precious gift from his old flame Elise de Bragelonne which he, in turned, bequeathed to Albert Campion. What was it?
   Burgundy wine "Les Enfants Doux"
6.) In which novel does Miss Maud Silver assist an heiress obligated to make an annual will?
   "Lonesome Road"
7.) Lord Peter Wimsey helps Hannah Marryat find the will for a 250,000 pound sterling estate. Where had her uncle hidden the clue?
   In a crossword puzzle on the floor of the impluvium.

8.) After having known Lady Amanda Fitton for one week Albert Campion named her beneficiary on his insurance policy. For how much?
50,000 pounds sterling
9.) Lord Peter Wimsey claims to be writing a book about interesting wills entitled what?
"Clauses and Consequences"
10.) Great-Uncle Joseph Ferguson (a suicide at age 95) bequeathed.. what? to his Medical Student nephew Thomas MacPherson?
His stomach, which contained pearls.

ANSWERS
Chapter 29 – About the Authors

1.) She was born.. when?
    1.) 1890
    Agatha Christie
    2.) 1893
    Dorothy L. Sayers
    3.) 1899
    Ngaio Marsh
    4.) 1904
    Margery Allingham
    5.) 1878
    Patricia Wentworth
    6.) 1896
    Josephine Tey

2.) She was born.. where?
    1.) Christchurch, New Zealand
    Ngaio Marsh
    2.) Torquay, England
    Agatha Christie
    3.) Scotland
    Josephine Tey
    4.) East Anglia, England
    Dorothy L. Sayers
    5.) Mussoorie, India
    Patricia Wentworth

3.) Who is she *Also Known As* ?
    1.) Elizabeth McIntosh
    Josephine Tey
    2.) Mrs Max Mallowan
    Agatha Christie

3.) Edith
Ngaio Marsh
4.) Mrs Fleming
Dorothy L. Sayers
5.) Dora Amy Elles Dillon Turnbull
Patricia Wentworth
6.) Mrs Phillip Youngman Carter
Margery Allingham
7.) Mary Westmacott
Agatha Christie
8.) Gordon Daviot
Josephine Tey
9.) Maxwell March
Margery Allingham

4.) Small Scandals.. who?
    1.) Her second husband was 20 years her junior.
Agatha Christie
    2.) She bore an illegitimate son.
Dorothy L. Sayers
    3.) When located, after several days disappearance, who was registered in a hotel using the name of her husband's mistress.
Agatha Christie

5.) Her First Whodunit.. was?
    1.) A Man Lay Dead
Ngaio Marsh
    2.) The White Cottage Mystery
Margery Allingham
    3.) The Astonishing Adventure of Jane Smith
Patricia Wentworth

4.) The Corpse in the Bathtub
Dorothy L. Sayers
5.) The Mysterious Affair at Styles
Agatha Christie

6.) Her Last Whodunit.. was?
    1.) Light Thickens
Ngaio Marsh
    2.) A Cargo of Eagles
Margery Allingham
    3.) Elephants can Remember
Agatha Christie

7.) She worked as a.. what?
    1.) Hospital Dispensary Clerk
Agatha Christie
    2.) Actress
Ngaio Marsh
    3.) Film Production
Margery Allingham
    4.) Theatre Producer
Ngaio Marsh
    5.) Trainee Opera Singer
Agatha Christie
    6.) Historic Writer
Josephine Tey
    7.) Religious Writer
Dorothy L. Sayers
    8.) Travel Writer
Agatha Christie
    9.) Advertising Copywriter
Dorothy L. Sayers
    10.) Landscape Painter
Ngaio Marsh

8.) She was awarded.. what?
   1.) M.A. at Somerville College, Oxford, reading History.
   Dorothy L. Sayers
   2.) Her "damery" for her work in the revival of live theatre at her birthplace.
   Ngaio Marsh
   3.) In 1956 the "Order of the British Empire".
   Agatha Christie

9.) She died.. when?
   1.) 1952
   Josephine Tey
   2.) 1957
   Dorothy L. Sayers
   3.) 1961
   Patricia Wentworth
   4.) 1966
   Margery Allingham
   5.) 1976
   Agatha Christie
   6.) 1982
   Ngaio Marsh

10.) Tough Stuff
   1.) She was killed in a car crash.
   Josephine Tey
   2.) Her father was an American.
   Agatha Christie
   3.) From what language does the name "Ngaio" come?
   Maori

4.) How many times was "The Mysterious Affair at Styles" rejected before Agatha Christie found a publisher?
Six
5.) Margery Allingham's first novel (published in book form in 1974) was serialized in what newspaper?
The Daily Express
6.) For what special occasion was Agatha Christie asked to write a radio play?
Queen Mary's 80th Birthday
7.) In "Death and the Dancing Footman" Ngaio Marsh refers to another Lethal Lady, mentioning that writer's book. Which author, and what book?
Dorothy L. Sayers "Busman's Honeymoon"
8.) In "The Body in the Library" Agatha Christie refers to another Lethal Lady when one of her characters claims to have the writer's autograph. Which writer?
Dorothy L. Sayers
9.) What is Agatha Christie's full name, including maiden and married names?
Agatha Mary Clarissa Miller Christie Mallowan
10.) In 1929 Dorothy Sayers put together the first major Mystery Anthology. What was it called?
"Omnibus of Crime"
11.) Whose hobby was motorcycling?
Dorothy L. Sayers

ANSWERS
Chapter 30 – The Really Tough Trivia

1.) What is Albert Campion's S.S.#?
   27
2.) In what magazine was Roderick Alleyn's home featured?
   "The Ideal Home"
3.) Whose phone number is 395?
   Jane Marple
4.) Whose phone number is Regent 01300?
   Albert Campion
5.) Whose phone number is Norwood 4380?
   Chief-Superintendent Oates
6.) Whose phone number is Sloane 84405?
   Roderick Alleyn
7.) Whose phone number is 21 Lenfold?
   Randall March
8.) Who likes "..weak tea with three drops of milk.." ?
   Frank Abbott
9.) What is Roderick Alleyn's favourite flower?
   Lilac
10.) What annual Christmas present does Alan Grant give his daily?
   a leather handbag
11.) Who speaks French "..in the honourable tradition of the Prioress in the Canterbury Tales.." ?
   Maud Silver
12.) Who likes a $3^{3/4}$ minute egg?
   Jane Marple
13.) What is Albert Campion's shoe size?
   Nine

14.) Where, in Suva, does George Alleyn live?
Government House
15.) Where did Tuppence and Tommy Beresford honeymoon?
Ostend
16.) Who is Jane Marple's favourite painter?
Alma Tadema
17.) What is Roderick Alleyn's morning paper?
"The Post"
18.) Who are Albert Campion's brokers?
Poulter, Braid and Simpson of Pall Mall
19.) When Tuppence worked in the hospital during WWI what were her bed rows?
A and B
20.) Who does Lugg call *"..The Prince of Parkhurst.."* ?
Roger Branch *(a butler)*
21.) What did Albert Campion store in Theo Bush's Museum of Wine?
"..an heirloom half-bottle of Grandfather's Dream.."
22.) Name the 85-to-1 winner of the St Leger in Doncaster.
Amateur
23.) Where does Inspector Fox go for his annual holiday?
Birchington
24.) Agatha Christie brought Hercule Poirot to the stage in what play?
"Black Coffee"

ANSWERS
Chapter 31 – Fun With Book Titles

Numbers Game - List all (or any) of the books with the following numbers in their title:

1.) 0
"Towards Zero"
"And Then There Were None" *(well if you want to get technical..)*
2.) 1
"One, Two Buckle My Shoe"
3.) 2
"One, Two Buckle My Shoe"
"Take Two at Bedtime"
4.) 3
"Three Blind Mice"
"Murder in Three Acts"
"Three-Act Tragedy"
"Third Girl" *(OK, this is stretching things a bit..)*
5.) 4
"The Big Four"
"4:50 from Paddington"
6.) 5
"Five Little Pigs"
"The Five Red Herrings"
7.) 6
None
8.) 7
"The Seven Dials Mystery"
9.) 8
None
10.) 9
"The Nine Tailors"

11.) 10
"Ten Were Missing"
plus there are another two and both start with "10 Little.." but continue with words that are no longer acceptable to publish.

Colour Scheme - *List all (or any) of the books with the following colours in their title:*

12.) Black
"Black As He's Painted"
"The Crime at Black Dudley"
"Black Plumes"
13.) White
"The White Cottage Mystery"
"Death in a White Tie"
14.) Ivory
"The Ivory Dagger"
15.) Brown
"The Man in the Brown Suit"
16.) Gray or Grey
"Grey Mask"
17.) Blue
"Mystery of the Blue Train"
18.) Red
"The Five Red Herrings"
19.) Green
"Mystery *(or Murder)* at Littlegreen House"

Where in the World? Identify the place in the title:

20.) "4:50 from **Paddington**"

21.) "Murder on the **Calais** Coach"
22.) "Murder on the **Orient** Express"
23.) "The Tiger in the **Smoke**" *(trick question! it means London)*
24.) "Passenger to **Frankfurt**"
25.) "They Came to **Baghdad**"
26.) "Death on the **Nile**"

Who said that? Identify the <u>source of the quotation</u> in the title:

27.) The Moving Finger
"The Rubaiyat of Omar Khayam"
28.) The Mirror Crack'd from Side to Side
"The Lady of Shallot" by Alfred, Lord Tennyson
29.) The Labours of Hercules
Greek Mythology
30.) The Singing Sands
Scottish Folk Song
31.) By the Pricking of my Thumbs
Shakespeare
32.) The Pale Horse
The Bible
33.) There is a Tide
Shakespeare
34.) Sad Cypress
Shakespeare
35.) Postern of Fate
"The Gates of Damascus" by James Elroy Flecker
36.) More Work for the Undertaker
18th Century Music Hall Song

ANSWERS
Chapter 32 – Novels "*Also Known As*"

1.) Alibi
   "The Murder of Roger Ackroyd"
2.) And Then There Were None
   "The Nursery-Rhyme Murders"
   "Ten Little.." (*two unprintable titles*)
3.) Anna, Where Are You?
   "Death at Deepend"
4.) An Overdose Of Death
   "One Two Buckle my Shoe"
   "The Patriotic Murders"
5.) A Surfeit Of Lampreys
   "Death of a Peer"
6.) A Wreath For Rivera
   "Swing Brother, Swing"
7.) Blood Will Tell
   "Mrs McGinty's Dead"
8.) The Boomerang Clue
   "Why didn't they ask Evans?"
9.) Brat Farrar
   "Come and Kill Me"
10.) The Bride of Death
   "Spinsters in Jeopardy"
11.) Come And Be Hanged
   "Towards Zero"
12.) Coroner's Pidgin
   "Pearls before Swine"
13.) The Corpse In The Bathtub
   "Whose Body?"
14.) Dancers in Mourning
   "Who Killed Chloe?"
15.) Danger Point

"In The Balance"
16.) Dark Threat
"Pilgrim's Rest"
17.) The Dawson Pedigree
"Unnatural Death"
18.) Deadly Duo
"Take Two at Bedtime"
19.) Death Of A Fool
"Off with His Head"
20.) Destination Unknown
"So Many Steps to Death"
21.) Dumb Witness
"Mystery *(or Murder)* at Littlegreen House"
"Poirot Loses a Client"
22.) Eyewitness To Murder
"4:50 from Paddington"
"Murder She Said"
"What Mrs McGillicuddy Saw"
23.) The Fear Sign
"Kingdom of Death"
"Sweet Danger"
24.) Five Little Pigs
"Go back for Murder"
"Murder in Retrospect"
25.) Five Red Herrings
"Suspicious Characters"
26.) Flowers for the Judge
"Legacy in Blood"
27.) The Gazebo
"The Summerhouse"
28.) Gyrth Chalice Mystery
"Look to the Lady"
29.) Hercule Poirot's Christmas

    "Holiday for Murder"
    "Murder for Christmas"
30.) Hide My Eyes
    "Ten Were Missing"
    "Tether's End"
31.) The Hollow
    "Murder after Hours"
32.) Killer in the Crowd
    "The Man in the Queue"
33.) Lord Edgeware Dies
    "Thirteen at Dinner"
34.) The Mousetrap
    "Three Blind Mice"
35.) Murder After Hours
    "The Hollow"
36.) Murder At Hazelmoor
    "The Sittaford Mystery"
37.) Murder in the Calais Coach
    "Murder on the Orient Express"
38.) Night At The Vulcan
    "Opening Night"
39.) Out of the Past
    "She Came Back"
    "The Traveller Returns"
40.) Remembered Death
    "Sparkling Cyanide"
41.) The Sabotage Murder Mystery
    "Traitor's Purse"
42.) Spotlight
    "The Wicked Uncle"
43.) Taken At The Flood
    "There is a Tide"
44.) The Thirteen Problems
    "The Tuesday Club Murders"

Works of Margery Allingham

1928 The White Cottage Mystery

Albert Campion
1929 The Crime at Black Dudley
aka The Black Dudley Murder
1929 Mystery Mile
1931 Look to the Lady
aka The Gyrth Chalice Mystery
1931 Police at the Funeral
1933 Sweet Danger
aka The Fear Sign
aka Kingdom of Death
1934 Death of a Ghost
1936 Flowers for the Judge
aka Legacy in Blood
1937 Mr Campion and Others
aka Mr Campion, Criminologist
1937 The Case of the Late Pig
1937 Dancers in Mourning
aka Who Killed Chloe?
1938 The Fashion in Shrouds
1940 Black Plumes
1941 Traitor's Purse
aka The Sabotage Murder Mystery
1945 Coroner's Pidgin
aka Pearls Before Swine
1947 Casebook of Mr Campion
1948 More Work for the Undertaker
1952 The Tiger in the Smoke
1955 The Beckoning Lady
aka The Estate of the Beckoning Lady

1958 Hide My Eyes
aka Tether's End
aka Ten Were Missing
1962 China Governess
1963 The Mysterious Mr Campion
1965 The Mind Readers
1968 A Cargo of Eagles
1969 Mr Campion's Farthing
1970 Mr Campion's Quarry
aka Mr Campion's Falcon
1989 The Return of Mr Campion
1992 Mr Campion's Lucky Day: And Other Stories

Mystery Short Stories
-A Matter of Form
-A Quarter of a Million
-The Barbarian
-The Beauty King
-Bird Thou Never Wert
-The Black Tent
-The Borderline Case
-The Case is Altered
-The Case of the Late Pig
-The Case of the White Elephant
-The Correspondents<
-The Curious Affair in Nut Row
-The Danger Point
-The Definite Article
-The Dog Day
-Evidence in Camera
-Face Value
-The Frenchman's Gloves
-Happy Christmas

- The Hat Trick
- He Preferred Them Sad
- He Was Asking After You
- Is There a Doctor in the House?
- Joke Over
- The Kernel of Truth
- The Lieabout
- Little Miss Know-All
- The Longer View
- The Lying-In-State
- The Man with the Sack
- The Meaning of the Act
- The Mind's Eye Mystery
- Mr Campion's Lucky Day
- Mum Knows Best
- Murder under the Mistletoe
- The Name on the Wrapper
- The Old Man in the Window
- Once in a Lifetime
- On Christmas Day in the Morning
- One Morning They'll Hang Him
- The Perfect Butler
- The Pioneers
- The Pro and the Con
- The Psychologist
- Publicity
- The Question Mark
- Safe as Houses
- The Same to Us
- The Secret
- The Sexton's Wife
- She Heard it on the Radio
- The Snapdragon and the C.I.D.
- Sweet and Low

-Tall Story
-They Never Get Caught
-Three is a Lucky Number
-'Tis Not Hereafter
-The Unseen Door
-The Villa Marie Celeste
-The Widow
-The Wind Glass
-The Wink
-The Wisdom of Esdras

Works of Agatha Christie

Hercule Poirot
1920 The Mysterious Affair at Styles
1923 Murder on the Links
1925 Poirot Investigates
1926 The Murder of Roger Ackroyd
aka Alibi
1927 The Big Four
1928 The Mystery of the Blue Train
1932 Peril at End House
1933 Lord Edgeware Dies
aka Thirteen at Dinner
1934 Murder on the Orient Express
aka Murder in the Calais Coach
1934 Three-Act Tragedy
aka Murder in Three Acts
1935 Death in the Clouds
aka Death in the Air
1935 The ABC Murders
aka The Alphabet Murders
1936 Cards on the Table
1936 Murder in Mesopotamia
1937 Death on the Nile
aka Murder on the Nile
1937 Dumb Witness
aka Poirot Loses a Client
aka Murder at Littlegreen House
aka Mystery at Littlegreen House
1937 Murder in the Mews
aka Dead Man's Mirror
1938 Appointment with Death
1938 Hercule Poirot's Christmas
aka A Holiday for Murder

aka Murder for Christmas
1940 Sad Cypress
1940 One, Two Buckle My Shoe
aka The Patriotic Murders
aka An Overdose of Death
1941 Evil Under the Sun
1943 Five Little Pigs
aka Murder in Retrospect
aka Go Back for Murder
1946 The Hollow
aka Murder After Hours
1947 The Labours of Hercules
1948 Taken at the Flood
aka There is a Tide
1952 Mrs McGinty's Dead
aka Blood Will Tell
1953 After the Funeral
aka Funerals are Fatal
1955 Hickory, Dickory Dock
aka Hickory, Dickory Death
1956 Dead Man's Folly
1959 Cat Among the Pigeons
1963 The Clocks
1967 Third Girl
1969 Hallowe'en Party
1972 Elephants Can Remember
1974 Poirot's Early Cases
aka Hercule Poirot's Early Cases
1975 Curtain *(written approx 1939-41)*
1984 Hercule Poirot's Casebook

Tommy and Tuppence Beresford
1922 The Secret Adversary
1929 Partners in Crime

1941 N or M?
1968 By the Pricking of my Thumbs
1973 Postern of Fate

Ariadne Oliver, Superintendent Battle, Mr Harley Quin, Mr Satterthwaite, and Mr Parker Pyne
1925 The Secret of Chimneys
1929 The Seven Dials Mystery
1930 The Mysterious Mr Quin
aka Passing of Mr Quin
1934 Parker Pyne Investigates
aka Parker Pyne, Detective
1936 Cards on the Table
1939 Easy to Kill
aka Murder is Easy
1944 Towards Zero
aka Come and Be Hanged

Miss Jane Marple
1928 The Tuesday Club Murders
aka The Thirteen Problems
1930 Murder at the Vicarage
1942 The Body in the Library
1943 The Moving Finger
1950 A Murder is Announced
1952 They Do It With Mirrors
aka Murder With Mirrors
1953 A Pocketful of Rye
1957 4:50 From Paddington
aka What Mrs McGillicuddy Saw
aka Eyewitness to Murder
aka Murder, She Said
1962 The Mirror Crack'd

aka The Mirror Crack'd from Side to Side
1964 A Caribbean Mystery
1965 At Bertram's Hotel
1971 Nemesis
1976 Sleeping Murder
1979 Miss Marple's Final Cases
1985 Miss Marple's Complete Stories

Mystery Short Stories
-Accident
-The Adventure of the Cheap Flat
-The Adventure of the Christmas Pudding
-The Adventure of the Clapham Cook
-The Adventure of the Egyptian Tomb
-The Adventure of the Italian Nobleman
-The Adventure of the Sinister Stranger
-The Adventure of the Western Star
-The Adventures of Johnnie Waverly
-The Affair at the Bungalow
-The Affair at the Victory Ball
-The Affair of the Pink Pearl
-The Ambassador's Boots
-The Apples of Hesperides
-The Arcadian Deer
-At the Bells and Motley
-The Augean Stables
-The Bird with the Broken Wing
-Blindman's Buff
-The Bloodstained Pavement
-The Blue Geranium
-The Call of Wings
-The Capture of Cerberus
-The Case of the Caretaker
-The Case of the City Clerk

-The Case of the Discontented Husband
-The Case of the Discontented Soldier
-The Case of the Distressed Lady
-The Case of the Middle-Aged Wife
-The Case of the Missing Lady
aka The Disappearance of Mrs Leigh-Gordon
-The Case of the Missing Will
-The Case of the Perfect Maid
-The Case of the Rich Woman
-The Chocolate Box
-A Christmas Tragedy
-The Clergyman's Daughter
-The Coming of Mr Quin
-The Companion
-The Cornish Mystery
-The Crackler
-The Cretan Bull
-The Dead Harlequin
-Dead Man's Mirror
-Death by Drowning
-Death on the Nile
-The Disappearance of Mr Davenheim
-The Double Clue
-Double Sin
-The Dream
-The Dressmaker's Doll
-The Erymanthian Boar
-A Fairy in the Flat
-The Face of Helen
-Finessing the King
-The Flock of Geryon
-Four and Twenty Blackbirds
-The Four Suspects
-The Fourth Man

- A Fruitful Sunday
- The Gate of Baghdad
- The Gentleman Dressed in Newspaper
- The Girdle of Hyppolita
- The Girl in the Train
- The Golden Ball
- Greenshaw's Folly
- Gypsy
- Harlequin's Lane
- Have you got everything you want?
- The Herb of Death
- The Horse of Diomedes
- The Hound of Death
- The House at Shiraz
- The House of Lurking Death
- How does your Garden Grow?
- The Idol House of Astarte
- In a Glass Darkly
- The Incredible Theft
- Ingots of Gold
- Jane in Search of a Job
- The Jewel Robbery at the Grand Metropolitan
- The Kidnapped Prime Minister
- The King of Clubs
- The Lamp
- The Last Seance
- The Lemesurier Inheritance
- The Lernean Hydra
- The Listerdale Mystery
- The Lost Mine
- The Man from the Sea
- The Manhood of Edward Robinson
- The Man in the Mist
- The Man who was No. 16

- The Market Basing Mystery
- The Million Dollar Bond Robbery
- Mr Eastwood's Adventure
aka Mystery of the Spanish Shawl
- Miss Marple tells a Story
- Motive v. Opportunity
- Murder in the Mews
- The Mystery of the Baghdad Chest
- The Mystery of the Blue Jar
- The Mystery of Hunter's Lodge
- The Mystery of the Spanish Chest
- The Nemean Lion
- The Oracle at Delphi
- The Pearl of Price
- Philomel Cottage
- The Plymouth Express
- A Pot of Tea
- Problem at Sea
- Problem at Pollensa Bay
aka Siren Business
- The Rajah's Emerald
- The Red House
- The Red Signal
- Sanctuary
- The Shadow on the Glass
- The Sign in the Sky
- Sing a Song of Sixpence
- SOS
- The Soul of the Croupier
- The Strange Case of Sir Arthur Carmichael
- The Strange Jest
- The Stymphalean Birds
- The Submarine Plans
- The Sunningdale Mystery

- Swan Song
- Tape-Measure Murder
aka The Case of the Retired Jeweller
aka A Village Murder
- The Theft of the Royal Ruby
- The Third-Floor Flat
- The Thumbmark of St. Peter
- The Tragedy of Marsden Manor
- Triangle at Rhodes
- The Tuesday Night Club
- The Unbreakable Alibi
- The Under Dog
- The Veiled Lady
- The Voice in the Dark
- Wasp's Nest
- Where there's a Will
- Wireless
- The Witness for the Prosecution
- The World's End
- Yellow Iris

Works of Ngaio Marsh

Roderick Alleyn
1934 A Man Lay Dead
1935 Enter a Murderer
1936 Death in Ecstasy
1936 The Nursing-Home Murder
1937 Vintage Murder
1938 Artists in Crime
1938 Death in a White Tie
1938 Death of a Peer
aka A Surfeit of Lampreys
1939 Overture to Death
1940 Death at the Bar
1941 Death and the Dancing Footman
1943 Colour Scheme
1945 Died in the Wool
1947 Final Curtain
1949 Swing, Brother Swing
aka A Wreath for Rivera
1951 Opening Night
aka Night at the Vulcan
1953 Spinsters in Jeopardy
aka The Bride of Death
1955 Scales of Justice
1956 Off with his Head
aka Death of a Fool
1958 Singing in the Shrouds
1959 False Scent
1962 Hand in Glove
1963 Dead Water
1966 Killer Dolphin
aka Death at the Dolphin
1969 A Clutch of Constables

1971 When in Rome
1972 Tied up in Tinsel
1974 Black as he's Painted
1977 Last Ditch
1978 Grave Mistake
1980 Photo Finish
1982 Light Thickens
1989 Collected Short Fiction

Mystery Short Stories
-A Fool About Money
-Chapter and Verse
-The Cupid Mirror
-Death on the Air
-The Hand in the Sand
-I Can Find My Way Out
-Morepork
-The Little Copplestone Mystery

Works of Dorothy L. Sayers

1930 The Documents in the Case

Lord Peter Wimsey
1923 Whose Body?
aka The Corpse in the Bathtub
1927 Unnatural Death
aka The Dawson Pedigree
1928 Clouds of Witness
1928 The Unpleasantness at the Bellona Club
1928 Lord Peter views the Body
1930 Strong Poison
1931 Five Red Herrings
aka Suspicious Characters
1932 Have His Carcase
1933 Murder Must Advertise
1933 Hangman's Holiday
1934 The Nine Tailors
1935 Gaudy Night
1937 Busman's Honeymoon
1938 Thrones, Dominations
1939 In the Teeth of the Evidence
1972 Striding Folly

Mystery Short Stories
-The Abominable History of the Man with Copper Fingers
-The Adventurous Exploit of the Cave of Ali Baba
-The Bibulous Business of a Matter of Taste
-The Entertaining Episode of the Article in Question
-The Fantastic Horror of the Cat in the Bag

- The Fascinating Problem of Uncle Meleager's Will
- The Fountain Plays
- The Haunted Policeman
- The Image in the Mirror
- The Incredible Elopment of Lord Peter Wimsey
- The Learned Adventure of the Dragon's Head
- Maher-shalal-hasbaz
- The Man Who Knew How
- Murder at Pentecost
- Murder in the Morning
- The Necklace of Pearls
- One Too Many
- The Piscatorial Farce of the Stolen Stomach
- The Poisoned Dow '08
- The Queen's Square
- Scrawns
- Sleuths on the Scent
- Striding Folly
- Talboys
- The Undignified Melodrama of the Bone of Contention
- The Unprincipled Affair of the Practical Joker
- The Unsolved Puzzle of the Man with No Face
- The Vindictive Story of the Footsteps that Ran

Works of Josephine Tey

1947 Miss Pym Disposes
1948 The Franchise Affair
1949 Brat Farrar
aka Come and Kill Me

Alan Grant
1929 The Man in the Queue
aka Killer in the Crowd
1936 A Shilling for Candles
1950 To Love and Be Wise
1951 The Daughter of Time
1952 The Singing Sands

Works of Patricia Wentworth

Miss Maud Silver
1929 Grey Mask
1937 The Case is Closed
1939 Lonesome Road
1942 Danger Point/In The Balance
1943 The Chinese Shawl
1944 Miss Silver Intervenes
aka Miss Silver deals with Death
1945 She Came Back
aka The Traveller Returns
aka Out of the Past
1945 The Clock Strikes Twelve
1946 The Key
1947 Latter End
1948 Pilgrim's Rest
aka Dark Threat
1948 Miss Silver Comes to Stay
1949 Spotlight
aka The Wicked Uncle
1950 Through the Wall
1950 Eternity Ring
1950 The Case of William Smith
1950 The Brading Collection
aka Mr Brading's Collection
1951 The Catherine Wheel
1953 Anna, Where are you?
aka Death at Deepend
1953 The Ivory Dagger
1954 The Watersplash
1954 Ladies Bane
1954 Poison in the Pen
1955 The Gazebo

aka The Summerhouse
1955 Vanishing Point
1956 The Fingerprint
1956 The Benevent Treasure
1956 The Silent Pool
1957 The Listening Eye
1960 The Alington Inheritance
1961 The Girl in the Cellar

Resources Used:

Print Resources:

"Agatha Christie, Biography"
by Janet Morgan

"Agatha Christie, The Art of her Crimes, The Paintings of Tom Adams"
by T.A. & Julian Symons

"Agatha Christie: A Talent to Deceive"
by Robert Barnard

"The Agatha Christie Quizbook"
by Andy East

"Dividends"
Book-of-the-Month Club Newsletter

"Come, Tell Me How You Live"
by Agatha Christie

"Detectionary"

"English Country Home Murders"
edited by Thomas Godfrey

"The Floating Admiral"
by The Detection Club

"The Great Detectives"
"An International Treasury of Mystery & Suspense"

"Ladykillers"
from Mastercrime

"The Life and Times of Miss Jane Marple"
by Anne Hart

Mastercrime Crime Quiz (pamphlet)

"Ms. Murder"
edited by Marie Smith

"The Murder Book"

"Murder for Christmas"
edited by Thomas Godfrey

"Murder Most Cozy"
edited by Cynthia Manson

"Murder on the Menu"
edited by Peter Haining

"Murder under the Mistletoe"
edited by Cynthia Mason

"The Mysterious World of Agatha Christie"
by Jeffrey Feinman

"65 Great Murder Mysteries"

"Verdict of 13"

Online Resources:

Books 'n Bytes
booksnbytes.com

Fantastic Fiction
fantasticfiction.co.uk

A Guide to Classic Mystery & Detection
mikegrost.com/classics.htm

The Mysterious Home Page
worldcat.org/title/mysterious-home-page

Stop! You're Killing Me
stopyourekillingme.com

Wikipedia

Printed in Great Britain
by Amazon